MW01017366

AN ARTIST IN CORFU

Written and Pictured by Sophie Atkinson

LONDON

HERBERT & DANIEL
21 *Maddox Street, W*
MCMXI.

PRINTED AT
THE WESTMINSTER PRESS
41IA HARROW ROAD
LONDON
W

CONTENTS

LIST OF ILLUSTRATIONS

INTRODUCTION

WITH a story reaching far beyond history to the glorious myths of Greece, Corfu shared also in its Golden Age, and in the fantastic mediæval romance of its Frankish subjection. The little island has played its part in every period of history, and until recent years was an important junction for commerce, and a more important political asset.

With a beauty of scenery unsurpassed in dainty perfection, and a climate that gives months of exquisite weather, Corfu has been strangely forgotten by our generation, and one can get information of it more readily from the classical scholar than from the average traveller.

East and West no longer strive for dominance in the Ionian Straits, and with the changing conditions of modern life commerce has passed into other channels. The island stepping-stones are no longer needed.

The great Venetian forts are silent and dismantled, and the lovely circle of the bay holds only a few cargo boats, a passing yacht, a fleet of fishing craft ; at most, a squad of orderly warships, replacing the free-booting pirate-admirals who were used to find Corfu so rich a prey. And the oft-disputed harbour reposes under a clause of perpetual neutrality.

An Artist in Corfu

Torn between races fierce for power, or struggling alone ; ruled by some alien hand or abandoned to the varied hordes of pirates which ever swept the shores of the Levant, the Ionian Islands rest at last, a band of gems unnoticed on their wonderful sea. A modern writer describes that sea as of " almost incredible blue," and it haunts the memory, with its marvel of ever changing colour, as perhaps the most worshipful of all Corfu's charms.

Though large numbers of tourists land during the spring months, they usually make only a short stay, and cannot be said to know the island, glanced at hastily while their steamer waits. The real Corfu, with the tender beauties of its olive woods, the simple friendliness of its peasants, the absorbing loveliness of its light and colour, the fascinating variety and abundance of its flowers—these are known only to a few outside its residents, a handful of faithful lovers who return year after year for the joy of its climate and the beauty of land and sea ; for the freedom and simplicity of its life ; or for the winter sport in Albania, whose rugged coast-line and ranges of wild snowy peaks, only a few miles across the straits, make so sharp a contrast with the green luxuriance of Corfu, and are so attractive to the Englishman in search of wild fowl, woodcock and wild boar.

The late Earl of Carlisle has written * that " anyone who wishes to condense the attractions of southern

---

* *Diary in Greek Waters.*

Introduction

scenery, and see it all in the utmost comfort and luxury, need only come to Corfu." This is still true after half a century, and now that imperial and royal yachts have shown the way within recent years, the island will doubtless receive an increasing number of visitors. It will awake to modern life; it may even become a winter "resort" and turn affluent and disagreeable; though, as its attractions are solely those that nature gave, we may hope that only nature lovers will resort to it.

As an artist I give thanks that I was there before celebrity has more than touched the island, and that I was given such very delightful opportunities for seeing the unchanged life of the country, and enjoying the placid content and perfect courtesy of its unspoilt peasantry. I must confess that small children have already begun to cry " pendarra " * on those roads to show places where there is tourist traffic, and indeed I heard some rumours of a public motor service; but, taken as a whole, the island is mediævally untouched, and absolutely delightful.

One can wander unmolested anywhere, sure of a hospitable welcome in any village, and a kindly reception of the most primitive attempts at conversational Greek. On all but the chief roads the horses will still shy—disastrously for their loads—at even a led bicycle, and a stranger is one to be much wondered after.

The village dogs are the only disagreeable note in

---

* Halfpenny.

3   B2

An Artist in Corfu

Corfu wanderings. Fortunately they do not know we are no good at stone-throwing, so the action alone is enough to keep them at a distance, and, on foot, they need not be regarded. Only while bicycling they become a more serious nuisance, occasionally endangering heels or skirts. As the roads through villages are generally steep, and more generally diversified by ruts, dust and stones, one feels that dogs make the track altogether too sporting. Except for this occasional hostility of the dogs, bicycling is an altogether enjoyable way of seeing Corfu. The main roads were made by the English and are mostly in good repair. The extraordinary hills and passes are well engineered, and as the road bends and turns the variety of scene is ever a surprise. The long lines of the hills of Epiros * blend with the island distances, and one remembers only to wonder, that Corfu is but forty miles long, and twenty at its widest, such varied beauty is its dower.

I am not advocating cycling for itself in Corfu, but merely as the simplest way of seeing the island. For it needs patience and almost as much work with the hands as with the pedals. It is usually possible to find a boy to push a bicycle up the big hills (though sometimes he has to be shown how). But coming down, it is brake, brake, all the way, with a halt here and there to rest the tired fingers.

From an artist's point of view Corfu is a paradise

* The whole mainland is usually called Albania now.

4

Introduction

of most varied charms. Every glance, every turn, gives a picture. A dainty colour scheme of blossom and olive ; or a decorative panel of graceful coast-line and sentinel cypress ; or vast sweep of hills gleaming white, or cloudswept to richest purple.

The flowers alone would make a botanist forget his home. And the peasants are magnificent ; whether resplendent in festa dresses, their fine heads tired mediævally, or in the soft faded and patched blues and browns of their working garb,—they are always just right. And the songs they sing at their work have a sound of the ancient world.

All through the spring months the women are seen scattered in little bands under the flickering sunlight of the olive-covered land, while in fields and orchards the men swing the heavy " zappe " * in a grand line of song and motion.

At morn, unendingly fascinating groups pass swiftly to work, and at sunset straggle in long procession up the rough tracks and steep roads to the villages. The women are gracefully erect under the great burdens of fruit, faggots, fodder or olives which all bear on their heads ; tiny girls trot barefoot beside them, each bearing her little head-load, or leading the handful of goats and sheep which are the constant companions of the family. There is probably a baby pillowed in a wide margin of grass, vegetables, olive sacks, etc., on the donkey.

* Hoe.

5

An Artist in Corfu

The spring sunset touches the island to a jewel mystery of colour, to the hush of some pastoral of long ago. Verily, the twentieth century has not yet arrived ; the nineteenth has hardly been here.

Over the Albanian hills sunset marshals the clouds to the wildest pageants, fading to more mysterious afterglow ; the snows shimmer green and grey and dun in the twilight ; the gold and rose of the opal sky faint and fly from the creeping shadows, and lingeringly the sea surrenders its last hold of their glory. Now if the full moon rise from beyond those snowy hills, the beauty over the Straits at sunset becomes entirely unearthly. It may be that our world made spells like this when it was young ; and the Ionian Sea hid one of them, and has kept the secret to stir our duller age.

It was very good to be in Corfu in those months of spring. My friends', the Dousmani's, house lies above Gastouri, among the steep dropping olive-woods, high over the Straits. It is quite near the Achilleion, and has almost an equal extent of view. Each morning, over the keen-edged hills, level with my window, came the sun, turning the sea to blinding silver, and calling to arise and seize the whole of the glorious day. The air was fresh and crisp from the gleaming mountain snow ; the sky, infinitely clear and high ; and the whole world twinkling with sunlight.

Then, if the blossom would let me pass without painting it, I must climb craggy little Kyria Ki, to see further over a world bathed in sunshine, passing by the way some bonny peasant girl and her goats at the spring in the brushwood. Or we must tramp across the island to a sunny height over the Mediterranean, where hawks hang far below us, and a little golden bay becomes a theatre for dreams. And the scent of the wild thyme enters alive into the memory.

In early summer the wonder of the clouds vanishes, their last outposts lying faintly over the melting snows of Epiros; moist warm airs take the place of the inspiring spring breezes, and the sun rises and sets in fairy mists of rose and amber and pale gold. The wealth of woodland flowers, the golden riches of the nestling orange gardens, the shimmer of blossoms throughout the olive-covered land—these spring beauties all slip away. But the wonder of the high sunlight increases: it turns the olives into trees of rainbow hue, draws strange orchises from the parched waste, hangs royal blazon of purple vetch by the wayside, and the dripping gold of broom among the crags. It sets young fig-leaves like emeralds among their ghostly branches, and swiftly it awakens the vineyards, till the vines—the tantalising, unpaintable greens of the vines—have covered the earth.

It is a new order of beauty that appears now, when the whole island is bathed in light, and it is perhaps the most fascinating of all.

The atmosphere for all its brilliancy and clearness is never hard, and the olives which cover Corfu as with a garment filter the light very tenderly to earth. Their fine veils of leaves reflect it in unbelievable variety of clear and gentle tints. Only the crags and graceful peaks rise above this flood of delicate smoke-like green, a revelation of colour and light.

High on the hillsides hang the long lines of the villages in their setting of olives and rock. On little peaks and crags all about rise their simple churches, each with a little detached belfry beside. White roads wind to the distant hills. Wild thyme and aromatic herbs scent the breeze. The half tropical whirr of insects fills the air. A goat girl unseen pipes a shrill cadence from the scrub. And near and far eternally the donkeys bray.

Do not miss the great spring festas. Of these, the most worthy is the procession of S. Spiridione on Palm Sunday. This great saint, patron of Corfu, and on various occasions saviour of the island from Turks and other plagues, is on the anniversaries of these escapes honoured in a procession around the town; and the Palm Sunday (Greek date) thanksgiving is very fine indeed; done with sincere reverence, and a joyous show of mediæval vestments, standards, lanterns, and so forth. The spectators are not less attractive than the procession, for every peasant who can spare the time and afford the journey comes into town, and there is a brave array of the delightful festa costumes of the different districts.

All through the spring there are Sunday dances in the village streets, and on Ascension Day there is a huge

Introduction

gathering near the Canone, just outside the town. But this has become so much a townsman's show now that the smaller and more distant village festas are better worth seeing. Village weddings are also delightful to watch, with their quaint ceremony of counting the dowry, and their music and dancing and little processions.

When you most reluctantly tear yourself from the country, there are the queer old streets of the town to explore; narrow and dark and curly, arcaded in Italian style, and not badly kept, though the sanitation is—well, southern.

The men embroidering festa dresses in the queer dens of the Hebraica are most paintable; but I think one would need to be trained from youth up to stand the Hebraica. The open market, on the wide harbour front, is sweeter, with its gay piles of fruit and vegetables under awnings, and its breezes fresh from the blue world of the Straits.

There are often warships anchored in the beautiful wide bay, and their sailors mix with the islanders and Albanians who are always clustered about the cafés and shops; fine looking highlanders with grand carriage and most picturesque costume. They are usually quite tractable in Corfu, though troublesome enough to their Turkish masters at home. The Corfiotes are a mild and gentle people, very restful after the Italians. They will not even pester you to go for drives, and it is quite unlikely that you will be begged from.

9

An Artist in Corfu

When you have seen a little of Corfu you will desire to return for many years. If you are an artist you must! Are there not most wonderful olive pastorals for a Corot; beautiful peasant studies for a Millet; changing miracles of atmosphere for a Turner; and most Teniers-like interiors in hut and oil-magazine? And can the newest Spanish painter show more daring colour than that cluster of peasants, homing in flat blaze of sunset, along the golden cliff-side road above the shadowed valley?

The sportsman, too, desires another winter in Corfu. And the dreamer, surely the dreamer, must return to this land as beautiful as a fairy-tale, that calls its lovers back by scent of thyme, and iris shimmer of countless flowers; by crystalline air, and a magic of high sunlight sifted through the island's veil of olives; by wondrous blue hills, over, and threaded by, more wonderful blue sea; and by the charm of a peasant life that knows nothing of the modern world. "So and no otherwise" indeed, calls Corfu to her lovers; and to her gentle spell they eagerly return.

But as in the close cultivation of the fields around the town there is not room, and the rest of the island is not level enough, for a golf-course, and as there are no entertainments, casinos, or other pastimes of civilisation, it is possible that the restless traveller of the present day may yet leave Corfu awhile in peace for those who love a land content in its comparative poverty and with a beauty all unspoilt by modern development. To these I would say that the people are friendly and hospitable, particularly to the British ; the hotels in town are good, and the journey simple.

Corfu is only a twelve hours' voyage from Brindisi, or four delightful days down the Adriatic from Venice, touching on the way at Ancona, Bari and Brindisi. The long sea route from Liverpool to Naples in any of the eastern boats is also a pleasant approach, and there is an occasional Ellerman-Papayanni liner which goes right to Corfu *via* Algiers and Malta, while a broken journey by way of Dalmatia is the most fascinating of all. I once went in a tramp—but that is quite a different tale.

Italian is the most useful language, as it is spoken by nearly every one in town, and even by a few of the country people in the nearer villages. But French, German and English are also very often understood in town, while in the country the slenderest knowledge of colloquial Greek will go a long way. Now the rest is all in the guide-books.

FOREWORD

I OFFER this story of Corfu with apologies, for I am neither scholar nor historian, and with no qualifications and much diffidence take up a scholar's theme. I have gathered my account from the learned works of those who see and record the pregnant facts of history, but I fear it lacks the synthesizing touch which should make it alive and true.

The story of a small and much-contested country is in any case liable to be only a procession of events and characters, as of scenes in a pageant : a tale of conquerors, marking, it is true, the trend of the world's power, but leaving our stage again ere they have touched our hearts or possessed our minds. And the smaller the country, the more its history is interwoven with that of its greater neighbours. Corfu's history becomes merged in the history of the south of Europe, and the little island is absorbed by its strifes.

Through the sunny peace of its limpid air come echoes of nearly all the great struggles of Europe :—of Greek and Roman, Roman and Barbarian, of cross and crescent, and of Europe and Corsican ; but the echoes are outworn and faint, and they cannot stir the profound tranquillity of Corfu, now a very lotos land of peace.

Foreword

My warmest thanks are due to the friends both in Corfu and in England who have given such unfailing help in the making of this book, and without whom it would not have been written.

I wish to thank Mr. Miller also for permission to quote from *The Latins in the Levant*, and to acknowledge my indebtedness to the other sources from which I have gathered this sketch of Corfu's history. In addition to the books (a list of which is on the next page) which I have referred to for the story of Corfu, I have used Isabel Florence Hapgood's translation of the Orthodox Church Services for the chapter on festas; and a translation by A. S. E. Dawes of a little book on S. Spiridione by the late Mr. Brokinis of Corfu, for the history of the processions of the saint.

S. ATKINSON.

April, 1911.

List of Authorities.

Manual of Ancient History (Schmitz), A. & C. Black, 1855. *History of the World* (Smith), Walton & Maberley, 1864. *Murray's Guide*, 1884. *The Latins in the Levant* (William Miller), John Murray, 1908. *The Princes of Achaia and the Chronicles of Morea* (Sir Rennell Rodd), Arnold, 1907. *History of the Crusades* (Michaud), Routledge, 1852. *The Navy of Venice* (Alethea Wiel), Murray, 1910. *Venice in the 13th and 14th Centuries* (F. C. Hodgson), George Allen, 1910. *Modern Europe* (Dyer), George Bell, 1877. *History of Geography* (Edward Freeman), *Historical Essays*, vol. III. (Edward Freeman), Macmillan, 1879. *Venice* (Molmenti). *Cambridge Modern History* (Cambridge University Press): vol. VIII., The European Powers and the Eastern Question (Richard Lodge), 1904; vol. ix., The Napoleonic Empire at its height (T. Holland Rose), 1906. *History of Europe, from the Commencement of the French Revolution to the Restoration of the Bourbons* (Sir Archibald Alison), Blackwood, 1854. Story of the Nations Series: *Greece* (Schuckburgh), Fisher Unwin, 1905. *Lithgow's Rare Adventures* (1609), Maclehose, 1906. *The Shores of the Mediterranean* (Frank Hall Standish), Ed. Lumley, Chancery Lane, 1837. *The Decline and Fall of the Roman Empire* (Gibbon). *History of Greece* (George Finlay), Clarendon Press, 1877. *Fynes Morison's Itinerary*, Maclehose, 1907.

ORFU.

:etch map
ewing
neral arrangement
villages, roads & mountains.
aces visited ___ .
ther villages ___ .

THE STORY OF CORFU

I

THE story of Corfu and her sister isles began so long ago that they were ancient in myth and renowned for beauty ere ever the first dim nebulæ of history had crystallised about them.

From all the beautiful land of Greece it was Cythera that took to herself the legend of foam-born Aphrodite, and in that island a wonderful shrine long marked the birthplace and favoured haunt of the golden goddess. *

Ithaka is the "dear fatherland" of Ulysses, and Kerkyra (Corfu) itself is haunted with the Homeric legend ; Fano in the north is, so they say, "the fair isle," the "seagirt island set with trees," where the bright goddess Calypso so long held Ulysses in her toils· But this island is only a few hours' voyage from Kerkyra, and we may wonder, just a little, how Ulysses' raft, with the fair wind sent by Calypso, took eighteen days over the passage. Though the western voyagings of Ulysses thus invite vaguer theories than his adventures in the then better known eastern seas, Kerkyra is very generally identified with fertile Scheria, the kingdom

---

* Lithgow saw the ruins of " the old adored shrine " in 1609.

of Alcinous, and land of the oar-loving Phæacians. And truly no one could desire a more lovely setting than its shores for the fair legend of Nausicaa. It does not really matter at which disputed point the wanderer was cast ashore. In the north-east, the tiny hamlet of Kassopa, with the site of ancient Kassiope, claims to be the capital of King Alcinous, and home of Nausicaa. And near it I know a little perfect bay that could hardly have passed through the ages of fable without becoming foster-parent to just such a charming tale. For surely white-armed Nausicaa should have played at ball there, where a rosy flower-foam on knee-deep meadow greets the waves, and the fresh north breeze woos white crests from the sea.

And, at so fair a landing, homeward-sailing Ulysses could scarce have wholly regretted this last delay.

But there is a second claimant for Nausicaa—in Potamó, with its full stream near lovely Govino bay. And as of old there were three cities in Kerkyra, here may have been one ; and we are left to prefer which we will as the most lovely and most likely.

Myself, being of Gastouri by adoption, I incline to our southern peasants' version, which places the walled town of Alcinous on the peninsula of Palæopolis, claims Cressida's stream, opposite on the lagoon, for the washing of royal linen (" for the places of washing are far distant from the city "), and the shores thereby, —the old Hyllæan harbour, now shallow and reed-fringed, as an inland lake—for the bleaching ground of the " girdles and garments and splendid cloaks " and the playground of the fair-haired princess and her maids.

The place fits so sweetly with the Homeric story : one feels that Corfu to-day might well be stage for it still : the finding and succouring of sea-worn divine Ulysses, and then the procession home—Nausicaa in front, holding her mules to the gentle foot-pace of her convoy. They pass around the lagoon, through the fields and tillage of men, to the city with the lofty turret and a fair port on each side and a narrow entrance. That city is dust, but the way to it is still through fields and tillage of men, by the safe harbour for the black ships.

And still the orchards by the Canone are fruitful, almost as those famous four acres of the stout-hearted Alcinous, where the fruit never perishes, nor does it fail in winter or summer, lasting throughout the whole year.

The characteristic Greek independence goes back even to these Homeric days ; for these Phæacians— " nearly related to the gods, yet neither of gods nor of mortal men " ;—were defying Poseidon, their ancestor, in befriending Ulysses. The Phæacians dwelt apart, intercourse with all mortals was forbidden, yet we find them, true Greeks in virtues as in faults, welcoming this stranger (doubly interdicted in that the sea god's wrath for the Polyphemus incident still pursued him), and giving him no stinted hospitality, but a royal feasting and gifts richer than would have fallen to him at the sack of Troy.

And though they invited him to contest in their games, they were too courteous hosts to cap his wonder-tales of wanderings, as, sea-faring demigods, they might have done. But they gave him of their best, and by the will of the Olympians sailed him home in peace to Ithaka at last, asleep in one of those magic Phæacian ships, which compassed the longest voyage in a single day; steered without rudder or helmsman by their own proper instinct.

And so Ulysses goes home, and is out of the story.

But Poseidon caught his bold rebel children as they returned—for Zeus granted his revenge—and he smote them with tempest, and bound the swift ship in the sea while driving home, and made it a stone and rooted it below.

And there it stays, unmistakeably the ship of the vanished Phæacians, and enduring sea-mark of the vengeance of a god.

The first definite fact in the history of Kerkyra is its colonisation by Corinth, B.C. 735; and the island colony flourished to such purpose that within a century it had established in its turn colonies at Leucas (Sta. Maura), and at Dyrrachium (Epidamnus), Apollonia, and Anactorium on the eastern shore of the Adriatic, by which it enjoyed a thriving trade with the hinterland of Illyria.

In a way characteristic of Greeks, and following the

precedent of their legendary forerunners, the Kerkyræans began to kick against the parental authority,
and the earliest sea-fight recorded in history took place
between the Corinthians and their rebellious colony,
B.C. 665.

Herodotus, their earliest historian, charges the
Kerkyræans with such disloyalty to the national cause,
during the Persian war of 475 B.C., that their names
were withheld from the muster roll of Salamis. But
their subsequent character in history is against this
story, for they were better soldiers and sailors than most
Greeks ; therefore the alternative account of this
incident is more credible, as it is more honourable.
In this version, the Kerkyræan fleet of fifty vessels
was ordered to await the issue of battle at Cape
Tænaron, and then join the victors, so the Kerkyræans
cannot be counted responsible for its absence.

Fifty ships, even little ones, were no mean contri-
bution to their country's navy : Kerkyra in those days,
and indeed through many cycles of unease and vicissi-
tudes, was a wealthy and important community.
Important enough then to set light to the smouldering
jealousies and discontents which burst into the Peloponnesian war.

The beginning of the disagreement was again about
colonies. In B.C. 435 one of the ordinary revolutions
occurred in Dyrrachium. The nobles, expelled, en-
listed neighbouring barbarians, and the populace sent
terrified for Kerkyra's help. This being refused they

applied to Corinth, mother state of Corfu, which sent a fleet that the Kercyræans defeated. The Kercyræans blockaded the town, won another naval victory, and then both parties applied to Athens for aid. Athens was first for helping Corinth, but the bribe of her splendid harbour as a starting-point for projected encroachments on Sicily and Italy, brought Pericles to the side of Kerkyra, and sent a fleet, to decide a naval battle in B.C. 432, in favour of the island. And thus the war began between the rival states.

By the end of the Peloponnesian war the political importance of Kerkyra had passed from her, for in 427 B.C. a civil war of unparalleled ferocity had rent the island; Athens in vain attempted to restore peace, and for the remainder of the classic period little is chronicled of Kerkyra.

We gather that her material prosperity suffered little for this political insignificance : for Xenophon, writing of the Spartan invasion under Mnessipus in 373 B.C., records the high state of Kerkyræan cultivation and fertility ; so tempting that the invaders promptly lapsed from Spartanhood, were sated with loot, and developed a very critical taste in wines !

The eastern shores of the Adriatic, the thin line of Dalmatia, and the Ionian stepping-stones further south have ever been the debatable land of Europe. The farthest bounds of Greek civilisation were here, and along this line crept Rome to an eastern empire.*

---

* Freeman, *Historical Essays*, vol. III.

Early History

In mediæval days east and west fought just as fiercely for these outposts and harbours. It is not a happy fate to be little and valuable among large fierce neighbours. The histories of the Ionian Islands are even more varied than is that of many-mastered Greece, while politically the history of Corfu hardly touches that of the motherland until the union of 1864.

In classic times Spartans, Athenians and Macedonians owned Kerkyra in turn : King Pyrrhus of Epiros held its dominating harbour during his Italian wars ; and finally, tormented by Teuta, Queen of Illyria, it submitted, soon after the Punic War, B.C. 229, to the rising power of Rome, and became one of the first and most important stations for the eastward advance of the new empire.

In the noble bay of Kerkyra Augustus gathered his fleet for that great battle that gave him the world, and a succession of illustrious Romans visited the island on their main passageway between Brundisium and Dyrrachium. Tibullus, Cato and Cicero all saw Kerkyra, and on the authority of Suetonius we learn that Nero, on his way to Greece, sang and danced before the ancient altar of Zeus at Kassiope.

II

THE MIDDLE AGES

The fortunes of the Ionian Islands again became troubled as the strong arm of Rome failed. The islands were divided among the various Latin states,

The Story of Corfu

and were desolated at frequent intervals by pirates of infinite variety, Christian and Moslem. Corfu and the island duchy of Cephalonia were the richest prizes, and their history rarely coincides, while at times the two islands have owed allegiance to powers as remote as Anjou and Byzantium. Summing up the changed times Gibbon* writes : " At the time of Pythagoras the coast of Great Greece was planted with free and opulent cities : these cities were peopled with soldiers, artists, and philosophers. . . ." In the tenth century " these once flourishing provinces were clouded with ignorance, impoverished with tyranny, and depopulated by barbarian war : nor can we severely accuse the exaggeration of a contemporary, that a fair and ample district was reduced to the same desolation which had covered the earth after the general deluge." Elsewhere he says, " The three great nations of the world, the Greeks, the Saracens and the Franks, encountered each other on the theatre of Italy." They encountered each other on the theatre of the Adriatic too, and Corfu was its key.

The Ionian Islands had their full share of chance and change in those amazing years of the Frankish conquest, when the restless energy and almost fantastic valour of a handful of knights-adventurers made conquest of Greece, and when the Fourth Crusade broke the ancient empire of Byzantium, founded New Rome, founded New France, but forgot Jerusalem. Swiftly

* VIII., 98.

Corfu and the Crusaders

the new kingdoms rose and fell, constantly their intricate balance was shifted by death or marriage or treaty, while the conquered people had scarce a word to say in the choice of their bold overlords.

Corfu endured much, for its superb harbour and defences and important position were always envied, and as dowry or dependency it passed under many hands. It had been mastered by Epiros, Achaia, Naples, Sicily and Anjou, before submitting to its four hundred years of Venetian rule.

Long ere the Frankish conquest of the Levant, the northern tribes had broken in on Romania; had become civilised, and been themselves invaded by northern rovers. The Northmen were seeking conquests, and the jealousies as well as the weaknesses of the established powers opened their gates :—as they opened them to the Saracens, in Spain, in Sicily, and in Italy.

Venice also was seeking conquest, the conquest of a vast commerce. A tributary of Byzantium in the ninth and tenth centuries, even then she owned and governed her own fortified quarter of that city; and her skilful commercial policy,* her ready navy, and increasing wealth, soon rid her of the most nominal submission, won her some of the finest defences in the Levant, and, in time, an almost crushing preponderance of trading rights in its ports.

* The policy of Venice was marked by the avarice of a trading, and the insolence of a maritime power, yet her ambition was prudent.— *Gibbon.*

25

The Story of Corfu

Corfu was a first necessity for the Levantine trade of Venice, and early she recognised this, but it was long ere she won the fort from its Norman lords.

In 1081 Robert Guiscard,* Norman founder of the kingdom of Naples, seized Corfu, with mind for an eastern empire beyond it. As type of the Norman adventurer at his best, this heroic master of Corfu is worthy of notice.

One of the twelve sons of Tancred, like nine of his brothers he wandered south to the Norman conquests in Apulia. Even the reluctant praise of his enemies has endowed him with the heroic qualities of a soldier and a statesman.

" His lofty stature surpassed the tallest of his army; his limbs were cast in the true proportion of strength and gracefulness; and to the decline of life he maintained the patient vigour of health and the commanding dignity of his form.

" His complexion was ruddy, his shoulders were broad, his hair and beard were long and of a flaxen colour, his eyes sparkled with fire, and his voice, like that of Achilles, could impress obedience and terror amidst the tumult of battle.

" His boundless ambition was founded on the consciousness of superior worth; in the pursuit of greatness he was never arrested by the scruples of justice and seldom moved by the feelings of humanity; though not insensible of fame, the choice of open or clandestine

* Guiscard = Wiscard = Wiseacre = Wiseman = Kallidus.

means was determined only by his present advantage.
... Robert was praised by the Apulian poet for excelling
the cunning of Ulysses and the eloquence of Cicero." *

The Pope had invested him Duke of Calabria,
Apulia, " and all the lands which his sword could rescue
from the schismatic Greeks and the unbelieving
Saracens." He had crossed to Sicily in an open boat,
and with incredible hardships and endurance in thirty
years had won the island. He had prepared a vast
force for the invasion of the Byzantine empire, and
Corfu was the first step on his way. The Greeks in
Corfu made no defence or opposition to the landing
of a portion of the Norman fleet, under Bohemond,
Robert's son, while along the coast the towns opened
before Robert's name. After a long and unsuccessful
siege of Durazzo he was summoned home by
troubles in Italy, and left Bohemond, a fine soldier,
to hold the Greek conquests.

This same year the Venetians at the invitation of
the Emperor Alexios Comnenos, attacked and took
Corfu, with the exception of the fort, stoutly defended
by Bohemond. Robert and a vast fleet were summoned
from Italy, there was much stern fighting, and a close
naval encounter in the " canal " of Casoppa.

Bad weather and the falling away of their Greek
allies weakened the Venetian fleet, and the Normans
finally annihilated it with the cruelty of the age, and
regained Corfu—with a raging pestilence upon them.

---

* Gibbon, vol. VII., p. 111, in Murray's edition of 1887.

The Story of Corfu

With Corfu as his base Robert made a second attempt on the eastern empire. He got to the heart of Epiros, and to Thessaly. He made Byzantium tremble, as in Italy he made the Emperor Henry fly before him; but he established no empire east of Corfu, and only held the island till 1088, when he died of an epidemic in Cephalonia.

Gibbon writes of this " premature death " at the age of seventy years.

He was succeeded by a son, Roger, who regained the Italian possessions and was made " Great Count " of Sicily in 1101, from whence he annexed ports along the African coast; but it seems Corfu had again lapsed to Romania, for when this great adventurer was re-buffed in advances for the hand of the heiress of that empire we find him breaking a peace of sixty years and sending his admiral George of Sicily to annex the island, which was done without opposition.*

Roger's navy was a growing menace to Italy and Greece, and only excelled by that of Venice, and the conquerors of Corfu soon made themselves so aggressive

---

* It is to be noted in the history of Corfu, how seldom the island alone made any attempt to resist a conqueror. Possessed by any strong power it was valiant to the death with its protectors; but left alone it opened willingly to the strongest. For its eternal choice was between the mastery of a naval power or the ravages of pirates. Gibbon states that when the jealousies of Italian states had let in the Saracens from Sicily, " Their frequent and almost annual squadrons issued from the port of Palermo . . . . and more formidable fleets were sometimes tempted to assist or oppose the Moslems of an adverse sect." Annual squadrons of Saracens; annual squadrons of all the other nations also, one may suppose, since they all came to the golden shores of the Levant to plunder and enslave.

along the shores of Greece that the Emperor Manuel was obliged to oppose them. But the Empire was suffering at the same period from Norman incursions at Thebes and Corinth, and poor Manuel could in no wise oppose these sea-wolves without the aid of the Venetian navy. The strong arm of Venice was, of course, ever ready, when concessions of trade or power were to be gained, and Byzantium's need was her opportunity for expansion in the Levant. Confirmed in the huge grants of honours, tribute and free-trade, gained by her help in 1085, and with the added concessions of free trade in Cyprus and Rhodes, Venice now joined the Greek fleet in a long siege of Corfu.

Though aware of the immense importance of the situation against the swelling tide of the Normans, for Athens, Thebes and Corinth were suffering from Norman rapine, jealous quarrels broke out between the Greek and Venetian allies. There was a shameful period when the Venetians withdrew, captured the Emperor Manuel and insulted him with a mockery he could not resent. Helpless, he could only beg them to continue the siege with him; and finally after a stubborn defence, the citadel fell in the autumn of 1148. This fierce struggle greatly augmented the growing enmity between Norman and Greek, Greek and Venetian, as the weakening empire felt the pressure of the younger powers. The enmity broke out later in a wholesale imprisonment of all Venetians in Constantinople in 1171, and an abortive expedition of revenge did not diminish the bitter feelings of Venice against Manuel. A wary hostility was offered by Venice to the encroaching western chiefs, whose tentative advances were threatening her eastern supremacy. The navy of Roger was second only to her own and in 1156 Normans and Greeks made a peace that lasted thirty years. The Adriatic was covered with the rival squadrons of Roger and Venice. But the power of the latter, disciplined by a slower growth, endured; while the Norman shrank and vanished.

In 1185 there was a last struggle between Normans and Greeks, when William the Good, grandson of Roger of Sicily, laid hands on Corfu and other parts of the eastern Adriatic, granting them in fief to his admiral, Margarito, who as " King of the Epirotes " (the period is resplendent in titles) founded a dynasty which in Cephalonia, Zante and Ithaka managed to endure till 1338.

" For two centuries each spring and summer produced a stream of Crusaders and pilgrims " and many landed in Corfu to pay their reverence at the famous shrine of Our Lady of Kasoppa. It is said of them that, the graceless folk, they took unlawful toll of the island's goods too.

Our own Richard Lionheart stayed in Corfu some weeks before continuing from Ragusa that overland journey home which the Duke of Austria so summarily interrupted.

The earlier Crusaders had endured untold sufferings,

persecutions and extortions in their overland travels through the Balkan peninsula. Now they came to Venice for transport. And the great day of Venice came when she, imperious dictator of the Fourth Crusade, took for her spoils the keys of the Levant, and her natural sphere of commerce.

For some years previous to the crusade Corfu had been virtually dominated by a Genoese, Vetrano, described impartially as an admiral or a pirate—on the lines, presumably, of Kingsley's theory that a gamekeeper is only a poacher turned inside out, and a poacher a gamekeeper turned outside in. But this lord of a rival city can hardly have been at home when the Crusaders landed, for we are told that the Corfiotes received them as liberators, gave them abundant provision and the pasturage which was so necessary for their horses (how the Crusaders ever got their horses alive to the Holy Land is a marvel !—they took 4500 in this expedition), and that they were so pleased with the hospitality and pleasant quarters that their stay was prolonged for some weeks.

But in ease and idleness the disputes of this much-divided crusade started again as they had done during the previous winter in Zara. The malcontents withdrew to a secluded valley to discuss plans of secession. Their bishops and chiefs found them, and only by prostrating themselves with tears moved these dissatis-fied followers to continue the Crusade in some sort of unity.

The Story of Corfu

Corfu was the meeting place for the whole fleet and Michaud says, " The historians who have described its progress through the Archipelago, so full of remembrances of antiquity, have not been able to refrain from employing the language of poetry.

And here in the words of its own delightful chronicler, Geoffrey de Villehardouin, is the manner of its departing. It was Whitsun Eve, and Geoffrey " bears you witness that so gallant a sight was never seen. Right surely it seemed that this fleet was destined to conquer the world, for so far as the eye might reach was naught to see but the sails of galleys and of ships, in such sort that the hearts of men rejoiced thereat."

" The wind was favourable, and the sky pure and serene, a profound calm reigned over the waves ; three hundred vessels of all sizes, with their colours floating from their stems, covered an immense space ; the helmets and cuirasses of 30,000 warriors reflected the rays of the sun ; now were heard sounding over the waters the hymns of the priests, invoking blessings of Heaven, and then the voices of the soldiers, soothing the leisure of the voyage with martial songs, and the braying of trumpets and neighing of horses, mingled with the dashing of oars. . . ." *

Small wonder that recruits came again to this gallant armament which " intended to conquer kingdoms," and to these men who " feared nothing but the falling of the heavens."

---

* Michaud, *History of the Crusades*, vol. II., p. 77-80.

Michael the Despot

When in 1204 Constantinople fell to the allies, led by Baldwin, the spoil of Venice was " a quarter and half a quarter of the whole empire of Romania," and the ever-crafty republic managed to include in that share Corfu, as well as most of the trading and strategic points in Greece.

This early allotment of Corfu to Venice was, however, like much of the partitioning of the empire, rather nominal than actual. It was not certain whether Vetrano was actually in occupation when Venice arrived, or whether the island was nominally under the empire. In any case Venetian and Genoese alternated several times as masters till Venice finally defeated Vetrano and put him to death.

Finding Corfu still too troublesome a possession for her direct government, she farmed out the island, for an annual payment of 500 gold pieces, to ten of her nobles—a common fate for the colonies of Venice. But even yet Corfu was not for Venice, for in 1210 that dominant and unscrupulous despot, Michael of Epiros, swept from the east, found Corfu a willing conquest, and established there a dynasty which lasted half a century.

The firm rule of these ruthless but capable despots gave a breathing space to the harried island ; while their powerful support of the orthodox church, recognised by them as the strongest bulwark against western invaders, laid the foundations of privileges which outlasted centuries of Angevin and Venetian dominance.

D

The Story of Corfu

It is doubtless due chiefly to this well-founded and enduring religious body that the national feeling and spirit have so wonderfully survived every foreign domination and kept Corfu Greek at heart perpetually.

As dowry of the beautiful Helen, daughter of despot Michael II., Corfu, with its dependencies of Butrinto, Suboto and Valona, came to Manfred von Hohenstaufen of Sicily (c. 1258), who took the title of " Lord of Romania," and allotted to his governor Fillipo Chinardo the task of reconciling the islanders to their western ruler.

Chinardo continued to hold his authority after the tragic end of the Hohenstaufen at Benevento, and it seems that wily Despot, Michael then endeavoured to secure an alliance with this strong man Chinardo by bestowing on him the hand of his sister-in-law, and Corfu, as a dowry, over again, since its legitimate possessor, Helen, was irrecoverably a captive.*

The Despot's aid was powerful but fickle ; he was soon intriguing against Chinardo in Corfu, and the pro-Latin party there invited against him the help of Charles of Anjou, the conqueror of Benevento. As the Emperor Baldwin also needed the support of Charles, the latter was confirmed in the overlordship of Corfu, together with the rest of poor Helen's dowry in Epiros, the principality of Achaia, and many of the islands.

---

* Helen's end was tragic beyond most. After Benevento, she was imprisoned with her daughter and three sons in the Castello del Parco, Nocera, where she lingered till 1271. Her wretched children then continued their living death in the Castel del Uova at Naples.

Roving Adventurers

A very handsome bribe, by which Corfu passed into Angevin possession, and in it remained for over a century.

By 1278 the Angevin was dominant in Greece, and he granted his Achaian principality, and with it Corfu, etc., to Florent d'Avesnes, a Fleming, on his marriage with Isabella, Lady of the Morea, and by a former marriage daughter-in-law of himself.

In the next generation Corfu was again allied to Epiros when Philip of Taranto, son of Charles II., married the Epirote heiress Thamar, and received from his father Corfu, Butrinto, and the overlordship of Achaia, for an annual payment of six velvet robes. Later he became suzerain of all the Frankish states in Greece and ruled Corfu for forty years.

Except for this period of Philip's wise and firm government, we do not find that her high connections with the paramount chiefs of east and west were any guarantee of peace and security to Corfu. There are *catalogues* of the pirates of different breeds who plundered these shores, and the fear of them even depopulated some of the islands. Roger de Lluria, a famous pirate-admiral of James of Aragon, appeared in Greek waters in 1292, ravaging Greek and Frank impartially, and dealing particularly thoroughly with the Angevin possessions such as Corfu, for the Angevin power had waned after the " Sicilian vespers."

The Catalan grand company, a vast band of mercenary adventurers bound for Constantinople (and incidentally the conquest of Boetia and the Morea) devastated this fair island of their former masters, the Angevins; while in these centuries, the schism of 1053 and the jealous Romanism of the Angevin conquerors put bitterer feeling into all strife of east and west, into the relationship of conquered and conqueror.

Corfu suffered, like the rest of Greece, from generations of free-lances, for by 1377 the Navarrese (Aragon) company was superseding the Catalan as dominant military power of Greece. They made friends with the Venetian colonies there and became masters of the Morea.

Frankly inspired by acquisitiveness, these roving hordes of adventurers must have been worse to bear than the Crusaders; for with all the faults of the latter their first aim was high and disinterested and must have drawn in a leaven of many noble spirits. It is difficult to imagine the condition of an often mastered land, such as Greece, abandoned to these organised robber rulers, and the offshoots of rebel robbers they would leave on their trail.

The empire of Romania was now being straitly hemmed in between advancing Turks, the great kingdom of Servia, and the western invaders. Greece proper had for long been hardly more than a shifting agglomeration of Frankish estates, held by personal prowess, and with little unity or political importance. The time was coming for these broken fragments of empire to be remodelled under the hands of the Mussulman.

Venetian and Turk

Meanwhile, in 1380, the Navarrese Company took Corfu from the Angevins on behalf of Jacques de Baux, titular Emperor of Romania and a nephew of Philip II. of Taranto. In 1381, Corfiote leaders arose against the Navarrese officers and offered submission to Charles III. of Naples, a safer overlord for these dangerous times. The Corfiotes must have been weary of changing lords and of suffering their deputies, and of the weak intervals when pirates ravaged.

In 1386, the " Captain of the Gulf," chief of the Adriatic fleet of Venice, took peaceful possession of Corfu, with the acquiescence of its leading inhabitants ; and so the island passed to the protection of the only navy capable of withstanding the Turk, and became one of the long chain of Venetian pickets running through the Levant to Constantinople.

At this period a very large proportion of the trade of Constantinople was in the hands of Venice, and she was determined to keep an open road to her greatest mart. Even after Lepanto (1571) the merchant republic signed treaties with the detested Turk, for continued trading rights. As Molmenti writes, with Venice, " economic policy takes the place of political economy." *

By 1400 the Turks were wasting the European lands of Romania. In the north the Servian empire was crumbling before them, till a century later they ruled

* *Venice*, I., 145.

to the Danube, with a vast tributary domain beyond ; southward they were reaching to the North African States by way of Syria and Egypt. In 1453 they held the heart of the Empire; by 1460 they held the Peloponnesus. Later, Otranto was in their hands. It was indeed just in time that Corfu came to Venice.

The bold minds and adventurous swords of western Europe were no longer set on carving kingdoms from the east : the Mussulmans were forestalling them there. Besides, Europe in general was absorbing its venturous manhood in wars of its own, or seeking southwards and westwards for new conquests and trade routes by sea to replace those seized or sundered by the widening barrier of the Turks in the east. Therefore Europe's interest in the great Levantine struggle was remote and of little practical help.

Alone except for Hungary, Venice, the sea-bride and sea-supported, held for her life the Turks in check with a fringe of desperately contested forts. And great among these forlorn hopes of Christendom stood Corfu, ancient in strife.

The rule of the Venetians in Corfu has been variously described as a ruthless domination of a hapless people, and a wise policy of development and gradual concession. Whatever their methods, it is certain that their protection was then necessary to the island—and the island necessary to Christendom.

As, century by century, the other great Christian

strongholds fell to the Turks,* Corfu stood, a firm and solitary outpost in the west ; and against its rocks the Turks hurled their last effort at conquest in Christian lands.

Their first attempt to take Corfu was in 1430, and their repulse then kept them from any serious assault until the famous siege of 1537.† It was shortly before this siege that the town, till then unwalled, quarried ruthlessly in Palæopolis for its materials of defence : a precedent for conduct that has left Corfu an archæological blank. But in the story of the siege is found ample excuse for any means of defence that came to hand.

This siege of Corfu is but a page in the savage story of Cross and Crescent in the Mediterranean. A hideous persecution of the Moors was disgracing Spain, who armed also against the eastern Turks for the fateful battle of Lepanto, and sent a grudging support to Malta. The Levantine forts each had their great sieges and were in constant strife at the Turkish frontiers. Before Lepanto, the Turks with 200 sail devastated Corfu and the Dalmatian coast. The French joined the Turks against Spain in Sicily, 1553. Such continuous presence of enmity and bloodshed is barely apprehensible by a modern mind. The fierce rivalries of cities, their intrigues and treacheries ; the straying companies

---

* Negropont in 1468, Lepanto 1499, Cephalonia, Modon, Corons Nauplia and Navarino 1500, Durazzo 1502, Monemvasia (the last holds of Venice in the Morea) 1540, Cyprus 1580, Candia 1669.

† See page 144.

of soldiers disbanded from the many wars; the armies of mercenaries; * the universal piracy. At some periods of the middle ages it is a marvel how anything but war ever got done. How anything was sown or grown, with serfs liable to eight months' military service in the year, from the ages of 16 to 60; how trade could exist and find materials for existence amid the constant bloodshed and raids and excursions! Yet in these centuries that are riddled with wars and sieges, and scarred with piracies, even Venice, the warden, found life more than just worth living, produced and enjoyed an unrivalled opulence of art, and grew even too rich for her absolute health—too rich at the last to seek her trade in the younger west: when the Turks barred her accustomed routes she fell to idle ways and an end of shame.

In that learned and delightful book, *The Latins in the Levant*, Mr. Miller has collected a vivid and inter. esting account of the condition of Corfu in Angevin and early Venetian years. Feudal service and usages were

---

* Roger de Flor, most popular of the Catalan chiefs, sailed from Messina for the East with 18 galleys, four great ships, 8000 adventurers, or, as some say, 6500, thus: 1500 men-at-arms, 4000 Amogavares, 1000 other foot soldiers, but this is not reckoning sailors.

"Venetian, Catalan and Turkish corsairs cruised in all the seas of Greece, carrying off the defenceless inhabitants to sell them as slaves. Some, in their eagerness for booty, paid very little attention to inquire who was sovereign of the country if plunder could be carried off with impunity. The Venetian Government excited the activity of its mercenary. troops by granting them two-thirds of all the booty collected, and by establishing regular sales by auction of the captives brought into the camp, paying the soldiers three ducats a-head for each prisoner."—Finlay, v., 63.

grafted wholesale on to Greece by the Franks, and the
elaborate system of its vassalage, the privileges of
the barons, and of the church, who stood so stoutly
to their rights, are all chronicled for us with
graphic and appreciative pen. We read of Isabella of
Valois and other noble Frankish dames on whom
the constant slayings thrust the leadership in
rough times; and we learn that Greece acquired
chivalry as well as feudal usages, and learned to
fight too, under its fighting rulers; and there is the
touching story of one of these rulers who rode into
battle with his standard tied to his hand, for he had
gout.

It is probable that Venice meant to do well by Corfu.
It is certain that she could not afford to offend its
inhabitants with the Turks at her doors. But Venetian
policy was always for Venice, and colonies and allies
might suffer any hardships if the Queen went unharmed.
The Greek colonies suffered more than a little: Corfu, as
as head, probably less than the others. She was the seat
of the colonial governor—"Provveditore del Levant"—
and of other high officials; petitions of rights had a
chance of fair hearing and of arriving at the home
government. The Corfiotes seem to have been fairly
treated on the whole by all their rulers, and both Philip
of Taranto and the Venetians were wise enough to
encourage the natural resources of the country. But
the short-sighted egoism of Venice counteracted her
good intentions in this respect. She prevented educa-

tion or made it a farce.* She divorced the gentry from their estates by forbidding them all trade and obliging them to reside in town if they wished for the small share of government allowed them. So though the Venetian dower of olive-trees tells a tale of foresight (for the Venetians gave 10 gold pieces for every grove of 100 olive-trees planted, till it is said, there were 2,000,000 trees before they left the island), the neglected estates, tended by undirected peasants, the aimless town life of the gentry, and the consequent stagnation of the once vigorous island attest to a lack of finer vision in the masters of Corfu.

Little except the soil seems to have received any cultivation or development in Venetian times. Small share of either fell to the inhabitants for all their 400 years of affiliation with the great republic. The people were humoured when possible : the gentry were kept loyal by a share in naval leadership,† or docile by honours and small place-holding. But with no worthy equivalent the latter were taken from their natural life and leadership. And they have not yet found their way back to it.

But nature made Corfu fertile in spite of all men's deeds, and it only needed the British rule to start the island into a fair prosperity.

---

* Corfiotes at Italian Universities were encouraged to take their degrees without studying for them ! while there were hardly any schools on the island.

† The Corfiotes shared in the war of Venice against the Turks in the Morea, 1463, &c., and along the coast, and even took vigorous part in the purely Italian wars of Venice.

Lithgow's Impressions

Before we come to modern days, however, I would like you to read how Venetian Corfu struck a contemporary.

Lithgow's *Rare Adventures* was published in 1632; its ample, leisurely spelling and sober pace give to our modern English a clipped and undignified appearance; and though Lithgow is a little careless in detail—*some* one has dragged in " Corsican," and the fortress rock is *not* a mountain, seen even from the smallest boat—I think it would be hard to improve on his candid record ; while his vocabulary is a sheer joy :—

" The Ile Corfu. . . . and upon the sixt day after our departure from Ragusa, we arrived at Corfu.

" Corfu is an island no less beautifull than invincible : It lieth in the Sea Ionean, the Inhabitants are Greekes, and the Governours Venetians : This Ile was much honoured by Homer, for the pleasant Gardens of Alcino, which were in his time. This Alcino was that Corcyrian Poet, who so benignely received Ulysses after his ship wracke, and of whom Ovid said,

Quid bifera Alcinoi referam pomaria ? vos que,
Qui nunquam vacui prodistis in æthere rami.

Why blaze I forth, Alkinoe's fertile soyle,
And trees, from whence, all times they fruit recoyle.

" This Ile was given to the Venetians by the Corsicans, Anno 1382, because they were exposed to all the

43

injuries in the world : It lieth like to a halfe moone,
or half a circle East and North. . . .

"The City Corfu, from which the Ile has its name,
is situate at the foote of a Mountain whereupon are
builded two strong Fortresses, and invironed with a
Rocke : The one is called the Fortezza Nova, and the
other the Fortezza Vecchia. They are well governed,
and circumspectly kept, lest by the instigation of the
one Captaine the other should commit any treasonable
effect. And for the same purpose, the Governours of
both Castles, at their election before the Senatours of
Venice are sworne ; neither privately, nor openly to
have mutual conference ; nor to write to another, for
the space of two yeares, which is the time of their
government.

"These Castles are inaccessable, and unconquerable,
if that the Keepers be loyall, and provided with
naturall and martiall furniture. They are vulgarly
called, The Forts of Christendome, by the Greekes ;
but more justly, The Strength of Venice : for if these
forts were taken by the Turkes, or by the Spanyard
who would so gladly have them, the trade of the
Venetian Merchants would be of none account ; yea
the very meane to overthrow Venice it selfe."

Even nicer is the account of adventures which follow
Mr. Lithgow's departure from Corfu. He passes
Sta. Maura—uninhabited save for Jews expelled from
Spain, and soon after Cephalonia and Ithaka are left

behind, we may learn from him what globe-trotting was like in those days (1609).

" In this meane while of our navigable passage, The Captaine of the vessell espied a Saile coming from Sea, he presently being moved therewith, sent a Mariner to the toppe, who certified him she was a Turkish Galley of Biserta, prosecuting a straight course to invade our Barke.

" Which sudden affrighting newes overwhelmed us almost in despare. Resolution being by the amazed Maister demaunded of every man what was best to doe, some replyed one way, and some another : Insomuch, that the most part of the passengers gave counsell, rather to render, than to fight ; being confident, their friends would pay their ransome, and so relieve them. But I the wandering Pilgrime, pondering in my pensive breast, my solitary estate, the distance of my country and my friends, could conceive no hope of deliverance. Upon the which troublesome and fearefull appearance of slavery, I absolutely arose, and spoke to the Maister, saying : The half of the Carmosalo is your owne, and the most part also of the loading (all of which he had told me before) wherefore my counsell is, that you prepare your selfe to fight, and go encourage your passengers, promise to your Mariners double wages, make ready your two peeces of Ordonance, your Muskets, Powder, Lead and half-Pikes : for who knoweth, but the Lord may deliver us from the thraldome of these Infidels. My exhortation ended, he was greatly animated therewith, and gave me thanks; whereupon assembling the passengers and mariners, he gave good comfort, and large promises to them all: So that their affrighted hopes were converted to a couragious resolution: . . . So they all set to work to make ready, each at the work and place assigned him by the Master, and the dexterous courage of all men was so forward to defend their lives and liberty that truly in mine opinion we seemed thrice as many as we were. . . . We recommended our selves in the hands of the Almighty: and in the meane while awaited their fiery salutations.

"In a furious spleene, the first Hola of their courtesies, was the progresse of a martiall conflict, thundring forth a terrible noise of Galley-roaring peeces. And we in a sad reply, sent out a backe-sounding eccho of fiery flying shots: which made an aequivox to the clouds. rebounding backward in our perturbed breasts the ambiguous sounds of feare and hope. After a long and doubtfull fight, both with great and small shot (night parting us) the Turkes retired till morning, and then were mindfull to give us the new rancounter of a second alarum.

"But as it pleased him, who never faileth his, to send down an unresistable tempest; about the breake of day we escaped their furious designes; and were enforced to seeke into the bay of Largostolo in Cephalonia; both because of the violent weather, and also for that a great Lake was stricken into our ship."

Lithgow's Impressions

It is all so simple, and so revealing !

Lithgow was a Scot, as dialect and character attest. He was travelling abroad because of some difficulty about a blood feud, I think. After this rancounter he had had enough of the sea ; besides, they had been obliged to beach the ship because of the great lake in her, so he decided to travel overland. And now we learn what were the chances of the road ; see, too, the haggard desolation of what was Greece ; and thereon receive gravely the epitomised moralising of our traveller :

" After my arrival in Peterasso, the Metropolitan of Peloponnesus, I left the turmoyling dangers of the intricated Iles, of the Ionean and Adriaticall seas, and advised to travell in the firme land of Greece, with a caravan of Greekes that was bound for Athens. . . . But before the aforesayd Caravan of Peterasso admitted me into his company he was wonderfull inquisitive, to know for what cause I travelled alone ? & of what Nation I was ? To whom I soberly excused, and discovered my selfe with modest answers, which pacified his curiosity ; but not his avaritious minde : for under a pretended protection he had of me, he extorted the most part of my money from my purse, without any regard of conscience.

" In the Desart way, I beheld many singular Monuments, and ruinous Castles, whose names I knew not, because I had an ignorant guide. But this I remember,

47

amongst those rockes my belly was pinched, and wearied was my body, with the climbing of fastidious mountaines, which bred no small griefe to my breast. Yet not withstanding of my distresse, the rememberance of those sweet seasoned Songs of Arcadian Sheepherds which pregnant Poets have so well penned, did recreate my fatigued corps with many sugred suppositions. . . .

" In all that country of Greece I could find nothing, to answer the famous relations, given by ancient Authors of the excellency of that land, but the name onely; the barbarousnesse of Turkes and Time, having defaced all the Monuments of Antiquity. No shew of honour, no habitation of men in an honest fashion, nor possessours of the Countrey in a Principality. But rather prisoners shut up in prisons, or addicted slaves to crude and tyrannical Maisters : So deformed is the State of that once worthy Realme, and so miserable is the burthen of that afflicted people : which, and the apparence of that permanency, grieved my heart to behold the sinister working of blind Fortune, which always plungeth the most renowned Champions, and their memory, in the profoundest pit of all extremities and oblivion."*

So Lithgow passed on his distressful way; and he is out of the story, as the sagas say.

Fynes Morison, fellow of Peterhouse, wrote an Itinerary of Travels in 1596, and his details complete the picture of sixteenth-century Corfu.

---

* Lithgow's *Rare Adventures*, p. 52 et seq :

Lithgow's Impressions

" From my tender youth, I had a great desire to see forrain countries," said he. And as a young man he achieved his desire.

" On Sunday the 5th of May we did see the Mountaine Fanon, (and as I remember an Iland) three miles distant from the Iland Corfu, and upon the Greeke shoare beyond the Iland, we did see the most high Mountains called Chimerae, inhabited by the Albanesi, who neither subject to the Turks nor Venetians, nor any other, doe upon occasion rob all; and the Venetians, and the Kings of France, and especially of Spaine, use to hire them in their warres.

" This Iland Corfu inhabited by Greekes is very fertile, yielding plenty of fruites, corne, wines, currands, and this Haven is fortified with two Forts cut out off a Rocke, namely, the old and the new Fort (which is more than a mile in circuit), both being very strong and held unexpugnable, so as the Iland is worthily reputed one of the chife Keyes of Christendome." *

After these two gentlemen I have little more to say of Corfu in the middle ages.

In the years that followed Lepanto, Venice and Constantinople remained at peace till about 1635–45, when the unabashed piracies of the Knights of Malta made excuse for the breaking of treaties.

Venice was again left alone to defend 1500 miles of sea frontiers against the Turk, and though declining

* Fynes Morison's *Itinerary*, I., 455 and II., 110.

in power and energy roused herself to her old valour for the splendid defence of Candia. The neglected defences of Corfu and Dalmatia were renewed about same time; for the Turks, though their territory was shrinking, were still formidable foes, perhaps more desperate in the south now that Hungary pressed so hard on their northern frontiers; and from 1600 Venice held in Greece only a few of the islands, with Corfu their only " unexpugnable " defence.

In 1716 the Turks attacked Corfu in force and both Venetians and Corfiotes gained glory in its defence : successful, under one of Prince Eugene's officers, Marshall Schulemberg. Finlay says, " It was the last glorious military exploit of the republic, and it was achieved by a German mercenary soldier.* Both Venice and the Turks had passed their prime ; world-power was making another step westward. The place of Corfu was no longer in the centre but on the fringe of the battle, and very soon she was laid aside from it altogether.

III

MODERN CORFU

When in 1796 young General Buonaparte led a ragged invincible army through north Italy, his vision was already of greater conquests. His pitiless betrayal of Venice to Austria was the price of Austria's acquiescence

* Finlay, V., 277. For account of siege see page 149.

to France in Corfu, and that the necessary prelude to French power in the Mediterranean.

For Napoleon, like all preceding conquerors, saw in Corfu his first step to the east. To Egypt, and an empire beyond, that should rival Britain.

In his diary he writes, "Venice must fall to those to whom we give the Italian continent, but meanwhile we will take its vessels, strip its arsenal, destroy its bank, and keep Corfu and Ancona." And again: "With Malta and Corfu we should soon be masters of the Mediterranean," and "Venice shall pay the expenses of the war."

Alas, poor bartered Queen and protector of the Isles. She paid in shame and bitterness.

And when they sacked her arsenal, it furnished out only two 64-gun ships and a few frigates. The rest of her once great navy was found unfit for sea. So Corfu passed to a newer naval power, one with all the will, but, as it proved, short capacity for holding her.

"I think," wrote Napoleon to Talleyrand, "that henceforth the chief maxim of the French Republic should be never to give up Corfu, Zante, etc. On the other hand we shall find these immense resources for commerce, and they will be of great interest for me in the future movements of Europe . . . if we are obliged to cede the Cape of Good Hope (to the English) we ought to take possession of Egypt."

In the next year Napoleon met Nelson at the Nile,

and learned that his way to an eastern empire was not to be through Egypt.

The Turks, alarmed by his aggressions there, had coalesced with Russia, and their combined fleets established a rigorous blockade of Corfu, where they soon ejected the sparse French garrison, and by annexing the island struck a severe blow at French power at a time when their losses were heavy in Italy, and just after their defeat at Aboukir.

The jealousies of the two new masters of Corfu were too acute for any united government, however. So Corfu and her sister isles were made into a separate state, under the joint suzerainty of Czar and Sultan, and with the title of Sept-insular Republic.

But though the French rule may have been a " hard and disgraceful slavery," the home rule seems to have been decidedly worse ; for within two years each island had been guilty of treason and rebellion against the central government, and local maladministration and anarchy had grown to such an extent that in Zante alone, with a population of less than 40,000 there was an average of one assassination per day. The principal islanders thereupon sent to the Czar a request for new and more efficacious form of government, which in due course was delivered to them in 1803. In 1804 the greater ambitions of France roused Russia to send a fleet and a fair-sized army to garrison Corfu ; but war was not made then, and the Republic continued until 1807.

Jealousies

In that year the Sept-insular Republic expired by absorption into the French Empire. Taken by the Treaty of Tilsit, together with Albania, Epiros, Thessaly, Attica, the Morea, Bosina, Candia, Macedonia, Dalmatia, and Malta, as the nucleus for a second attempt at eastern conquest. For this Napoleon's plans were all ready, and the very day after signing the treaty he issued directions for the massing of two armies in Italy, to be poured into the Balkan peninsula, one by way of Cattaro, the other from Corfu, on their way to the long projected Persian conquest. Writing to Marmont on August 24th, Napoleon says, " Understand this, however, that in the present posture of affairs, the loss of Corfu would be the greatest misfortune which could befall the empire." But Corfu was destined, in the end, to be of no importance to Napoleon, for the projected expedition was checked by a Russo-Turkish alliance, while Napoleon's attention was drawn away to the Spanish war, and two years later all the islands but Corfu and Paxos were peacefully " captured " by a British expedition under Lord Collingwood.

Paxos fell to us in 1814, and only the large garrison in Corfu held out another year. The town was strictly blockaded until the fall of Napoleon, when the Bourbons directed its restoration to the British.

In 1815, the powers, by the Treaty of Paris, made of the Ionian Islands a free and independent state under the sole protection of Britain. The command of " the

53

The Story of Corfu

finest harbour and the strongest fortress in the Adriatic"
had once more passed into the hands of the first naval
power, and the little island had peace at last.

The usual results of British rule followed in the
islands, order and prosperity, discipline and freedom
were extracted from chaos, and a period of tranquillity
and development commenced.

Sir Thomas Maitland was the first Lord High
Commissioner, and proved both popular and capable.
He was authorised to summon a constitutional assembly,
and constructed a very admirable charter, which was
accepted in 1817. By this the island gradually expanded
to a great proportion of self-government, and under it
enjoyed unparalleled prosperity. Justice was reliable
and uncorrupt. Taxation was light, chiefly in custom
dues. Life and property were secure.

The islanders were treated with a consideration
which must have been new to them after those turbulent
revolutionary years, when it was hard to tell who was
their master, and when mastery was only for profit and
spoil.

Education was provided for all classes, from primary
schools in the villages to the Lyceum and Gymnasium
in town. The Earl of Guildford founded the University of Corfu in 1823, but since the union with
Greece it has ceased to exist.

Material development naturally went hand in hand
with education. Excellent roads spread over the
islands ; harbours, quays and aqueducts encouraged

a vigorous growth of trade and industries ; while the large British garrison brought fresh life into the capital.

It is said that after the reform of the Charter by Lord Seaton in 1848–9 the machinery of government did not work so smoothly as before.

The peasants were not ready for the very extended suffrage and were unable to grasp in their true proportions the statements of the now unfettered press. In the same year in which their liberties were extended there was a rebellion in Zante ; and again in the year following, notable for its savagery.

It was in that first rebellion that the insurgents were held at bay at the garrison of Argostoli, and repulsed by twelve British soldiers under command of a sergeant. This man had the spirit of Hervé Riel ; for, being told to name his reward for the gallant defence, asked only —that his wife might be allowed to come out and join him.* It is satisfactory to know that in addition he received a pension (£20 !) and a medal.

In 1852 Greek superseded Italian as the official language. With increased education there arose a steady demand for union with the mother country ; a demand so natural and so insistent that in 1864 the islands were restored to Greece. The negotiations for this restoration were chiefly in the hands of Mr.

---

* But this was not so small a concession in those days; for in 1851 Lord Carlisle wrote of the Corfu garrison that only 6 per cent. of the men were allowed their wives, and "something yet remains to be done" for their accommodation, since they had to sleep in the common barrack rooms with the men.

The Story of Corfu

Gladstone as special commissioner, and Count Dousmani, at that time secretary of state for the islands, and were concluded by the Treaty of London, signed by Queen Victoria, the Emperors of Russia and France, and the King of Greece.

The unqualified union of the Ionian Islands with their mother country was most loyally and joyfully received. But it has been rumoured in later years that they do not always find their mother easier to deal with than their guardian, or more thoughtful for their interests. Lean years have come to the island, and it has sunk into a stagnation from which its intercourse with the wider range of Britain might have saved it.

However, now that Kaiser Wilhelm has adopted the Villa Achilleion for a holiday seat, and that Queen Alexandra also loves Corfu and visits it on all her Mediterranean cruises, the island is no longer in danger of remaining asleep, unknown, though modern commerce has passed it by, and its fort is no longer " the Keye of Christendome." Let us hope that its inhabitants will realise in time that untouched natural beauty is the sole, though ample, attraction of Corfu ; and that no vandalism or hope of gain may ever mar " the loveliest spot of all Greece."

Finlay states that the British rule in the Ionian Islands created misunderstanding and dislike on both sides. If so, that feeling is long past now ; the Corfiotes love of the English is only second to that of their own

Union with Greece

countrymen, and English people in Corfu are sure of the happiest and most friendly welcome. Enough time has passed to show Corfiotes the truth expressed by one of their own writers, Stefanos Xenos, who said, " If ever a state was prosperous, free and progressing under the dominion of another, that state was Ionia under the dominion of Great Britain ; and yet no people could be more restless in their position, and more anxious to escape from the shelter afforded by the patron power than the Ionians." *

Since the union with Greece Corfu has been happy in having no history, and if treaties hold, its stormy days are for ever over, for by the Treaty of London its harbour is guaranteed perpetual neutrality.

---

* *East and West* ; a diplomatic history of the annexation of the Ionian Isles to the Kingdom of Greece.

AN ARTIST IN CORFU

CHAPTER I

Spring in Corfu

IT is rather hard to say when spring begins in Corfu, for what we would consider to be the spring flowers—irises, anemones, etc.—come up most joyously as soon as the rains of autumn recall them to life, after the summer drought. However, they are still gaily flowering after all the winter storms, and woodland and waste are flooded with their colour through March and April.

These months are more passionately springlike than in England. A great gale tears over from Albania, flings torrents of hail and rain through the groves, rolls off in splendid masses of rainbow-shot cloud, and leaves everything twinkling more brightly than before, and the hills newly washed and wonderful.

The little donkey tracks, steeper and stonier than one would think possible for animals, will for half an hour be rather more watercourse than causeway; but the peasants will soon be at work again, indifferent, so it seems, to the drenched grass ; and the sun will be distilling double sweetness from orange blossom, and more exquisite fragrance from the lemon. Where'er one wanders through the woods, the air is violet-scented ; and from the first silver shining of the almond in February, there is an overlapping succession of all the blossoms, and a perfect riot of dainty woodland flowers ; the last of them holding out astonishingly into the hot-weather months, when one has just energy to wonder at their courage and endurance.

They make the island a fairyland throughout the spring. Under the olives stretch greenest glades all starred with mauve anemones, or blue with the three shades of lovely iris stylosa, whereof the two lighter shades are of silk, but the darkest of velvet. Even the daisies are glorified into shining patches of silver, and in the fields and vineyards shepherd's purse makes a right good show, or gives place to a rich patterned carpet of darling bird's-eye speedwell, tiny orange marigolds, the rosiest of silenes, cranes-bills, butter-cups, and pimpernels. All these colours are simply "laid on with a trowel," and above them are the deep purple anemones, or clumps of narcissi, ixias, oxalis and mallows, whose longer stalks raise them through the mosaic of smaller flowers. There are delightful grape hyacinths, too—drops of pure deep blue scattered in wayside grass and vineyard—and patches of purple honesty flowers in the hedges of thorn and prickly pear by the high-road. After the stylosas have passed, the woods are illumined by a very blue little day iris, a rigid little thing, in-dividually not so graceful as its predecessor, but very delightful in its mass of shimmering blue, and dying also in masses with wonderful unanimity. One after-noon I was trying to seize its colour and sparkle under

Spring in Corfu

the nearest olive trees. At about a quarter past four the colour dimmed, and within twenty minutes it had quite vanished, for every flower was shrivelled on its stalk. However, the spring flowers arose again and again in fresh beauty when one thought them gone for ever, and always some new arrival consoled for departed joys.

The blossom, both wild and cultivated, is a wonder and a joy, and demands imperiously that one should paint nothing else. It shimmers distantly among the rolling stretches of olive woods and about the hillside villages. It is arrayed in unimaginable glory of colour against the blue straits and mountains—a symphony of light, accented by the solemn tones of the great cypresses.

On sandy wild hillsides, from among whin and heath and scrub, the wild pears toss up long arms of foamy blossom ; more sheltered below is a thicket of blackthorn full of the sunlight. In the distance the young trees of the Cressida flats turn into a pink mist of peach blossom, followed by plum, pear, and apple, each in turn demanding the crown for beauty.

Later come the beautiful single-growing quince blossoms, the magnolias, so like white birds at rest, nespoles in golden knots ripening among their rich green foliage and taking the place of oranges in the colour scheme, and asphodel spreading like a fairy cloud through the woods. It is so beautiful, the asphodel : coming unnoticed at first, a poor-coloured

An Artist in Corfu

flower it seems, just like an enlargement of a London Pride straggling to three or four feet in height. Then one day it is no longer in single stalks, but a wonderful veil of rosy silver, possessing the glades of the ancient olive woods, a mystery and delight to the eye for all the weeks of its blossoming.

The charm of Corfu's flowers is not only in their splendid mass under that high sun, but equally in the dainty perfection of the little miniatures which reveal themselves in every rambling walk. Minute and fascinating members of the vetch and clover families appeared new to me almost daily; and the varieties of bee orchis are very beautiful and interesting. The favourites of cottage gardens and walls are carnations and stocks, la France and other roses, and wallflowers. In the courtyard the silken tassels of wistaria draped yards of the high wall, reached over and flung higher cascades of colour from the old olive-trees outside, and stretched a lovely pavilion over where the hammocks hung outside in the breeze between the olive trunks. The great purple irises filled all the beds in the courtyard at the same time, and there were pink tree peonies too, and feathery double dutzia.

In the long, fierce drought of the summer Corfiotes truly say they have no gardens, for water is always precious, and sometimes almost unprocurable; but during the spring months it is hard to remember this, for all the plants which can survive that summer

A GRAY DAY IN THE COURTYARD.

starvation grow with such beauty and luxuriance, that in their riches the coming lean months are forgotten.

The winter storms are generally past by the end of February, and a period of golden weather follows. Even at the end of June I did not find it too hot for painting, though I must confess that the donkey then bore me to work, and that from eleven till two I was happier indoors or in the hammock. Many Corfiote ladies say they do not begin to bathe before July, as it is *too cold* before then!

In May we used to go down to the sea at six o'clock in the morning, and even then there was not a shiver in the water, and the steep climb up again was much too hot for comfort. By June, in addition to the peasant girl bearing our garments, the procession included the donkey for E.'s return journey. I always found that at so acute an angle the exertion of sticking on to the pack-saddle on that minute beast's back was quite as great as walking.

In early morning the Straits and distant mountains are of softly shining silver—a most radiant mirror world. Strange fish swim unafraid beside one in the clear water or stroll with rudimentary limbs on the sandy bottom. Perhaps there are a few fishing boats afloat in the silver, or along the shore a band of men hauling their great net with a song. It is very ecstatic, but we do not stay long, or it will be too hot to start out for painting.

On some mornings I must confess the bathe seemed

An Artist in Corfu

rather a duty than a pleasure, when one contemplated the returning climb. But baths were a prohibitive luxury when the last rains had fallen, so it was sea or nothing. Then there were days of sirocco, too, sometimes, when one felt all cross and horrid, and there might be an invasion of insect life, when for a time Corfu ceased to be one's paradise. But the fresh north-west wind would come, and again the island would be the most lovely and desirable and bewilderingly paintable spot in the world, and a lifetime too short for its worthy admiration, as each day one's artistic desires so hopelessly outran their fulfilment.

I think the situation of the Dousmani's house is unsurpassed by any in the island. It is surrounded to its walls with olives and flowering trees and vineyards, and as the only road arrives near it from inland, after climbing the great Gastouri hill, its glorious view over the Straits comes as a breathless surprise to visitors. Like most country houses the ground floor is entirely occupied by the wine *magazine*—the large earth-floored chambers where the wine of the estate is made and stored—so at the first glance from the high first-floor windows one seems to be hung right over the wonderful blue world of the Straits. The steep-dropping olive woods below slide out of sight into the sea, and across the water the great white peaks and ranges of Epiros run southward to gentler slopes ;—to where, in the sickle's curve, our own mountains and crags drop to meet them in the slenderest point of Lefkimmo.

Spring in Corfu

Faint, beyond the Straits, on clear days a line of deeper blueness shows Paxo along the horizon.

The sea does not cease to be a marvel, an enchantress of subtle changing colour ; even on a grey day, throbbing with strange flushes of violet and veiled emerald, its harmonies of grey new to northern eyes, and hinting always at the masterful sun ; while on the usual spring morning, with a little breeze fingering its surface and sending along the bright clouds to enrich its melting blues with their pure shadows, not only ocean, but hills and woods share in the " unnumbered smile "—the sparkle which is never harsh and always luminous, and in which only the cypresses have no part.

One can be almost vexed one is a painter, so entrancing it would be to wander day-long in the green glades of the olives above the sea, and find new ways among their ancient terraced steeps. There, all through the spring months, the women gather ceaselessly the falling fruit, in gentle coloured groups of blues and browns ; not without some accent of red or orange in head-dress and apron, some movement of the accompanying children and goats.

Though the men have pleasant voices, the women chatter like gulls, shrilly and high. They give one friendly greeting in passing, with sometimes an offering of wayside flowers; and the younger women have a pretty habit of a violet dangling from the mouth, which makes their flashing smile additionally attractive.

One of the great pleasures of Corfu is the freedom

An Artist in Corfu

it allows to wander where one will. There are main roads between towns and villages ; beyond them only rough foot and donkey tracks among woods and fields and waste. Except for the multitudinous dry stone terracing, hoary and crumbling with age, for the olives on the steeper slopes, there are no walls, nor are there laws of trespass or custom to forbid one's excursions. Of course, one would no more think of passing among the young buds of a vineyard in April than of trampling June " mowing grass " in England; but with that exception the countryside is free for endless scrambles among the crags, through the woods, and down to the shore, where every fresh path reveals some entrancing view of land or sea or blossom ; some scene in the peasant's simple life ; some surprising glory of colour or light. And everywhere the soft green of the olives is over the island. One emerges from the spreading woods on to some great rock high above the sea, to look down upon this other sea of olives surging against the crags and cliffs, crowding round the villages, pushing almost over the shores of the island in its wealth of foliage, and turning to myriad rainbow colours in the intense light and air. The olives are the foundation—the dainty background—for all the brilliant beauties of Corfu,—as they are very literally its mainstay and support.

CHAPTER II

The Olive Workers

IN a good olive year the whole peasant population is absorbed by the olive harvest, which lingers from January till May, and is by far the most important crop for Corfu, furnishing practically its only export. For this reason it is to be regretted that the olive has not suited its internal economy to its responsible position. For it puts forth its flowers in April, just when it is most occupied with ripening fruit, so if its last year has been prolific it has really neither energy nor space to attend to this year's blossoming. Consequently its crops are very irregular, and the people dependent on them, at the best not rich, are in poor years almost destitute. It is said the peasants are improvident—but a diet of bread and oil does not leave a wide margin for thrift ! They are independent in some ways, possessing their little bits of land and clusters of trees, or renting them, at the price of a few days' work in the landlord's vineyard. They work freely and as they like, and are content in their little society and hereditary tasks. They rarely advance or develop beyond these ; offers of comfort, good wages and light work hardly tempt them from their fields to town or country service. They would feel as exiles from their kind, and would soon return to hard work and hard fare in freedom, to the pleasant evening gossip in *bottega* or by the well, and the friendly greetings in the fields.

Throughout the spring months the women and girls stoop and crouch day-long under the olives, gathering the tiny sloe-like berries and conveying them by head or donkey-load to the oil magazines, where their share of the work ends when they pile the fruit, still covered with grey bloom, into the stone bunkers which line the end of the *magazine*, to await its crushing.

The Corfiotes consider that the trees are harmed by beating, so until the final gathering the fruit is just left to drop, which it does steadily for months. After a few days of wind and rain have held the pickers idle, they have hard work to recover the quantity of fallen olives, which lie almost in masses under the trees, or are carried by the rains into every kink and pocket of walls and paths, making walking difficult, and sitting down impossible.

The oil magazines are part of every estate of any size. They are low, ancient and primitive stone buildings, with vastly picturesque interiors. Their small windows throw Rembrandt-like lights over the uneven floor, clumsy machinery, and moving figures, set in a most etchable mystery of shadows.

The Dousmani's magazine was the most fascinating place for wet days. There was little light, and still less room for sketching, but it was full of subject and character.

The Olive Workers

Under an arch at the far end are big stone bunkers, full of the fresh olives, which, with the patient pony in the midst, await their turn at the mill. Just opposite the door is the massive and primitive mill, formed by a roughly built stone bed about two feet high; and in its centre a great upright beam supporting a granite millstone. From the centre of the stone a somewhat slighter treetrunk radiates to be harnessed to the patient pony. And the mill's motive power is quickened by a man at its tail, who, as he follows round, shovels the olives into position or addresses himself to the pony as occasion requires.

He wears a blue blouse and the whole picture has the rhythmic monotony of a Millet.

It is Cipi, the overseer, who decides when the olives have been sufficiently crushed. He may take a turn at the mill; but is more likely to be sitting by the open hooded hearth, where a great black pot of water steams, with perhaps a smaller pan beside, into which he slices vegetables and bread for a savoury dinner.

On a wet day the women bringing in the olives wring out their dripping skirts and gather round the wood fire to eat their midday meal in shelter. Fine types, beautiful in movement and grouping, and strongly lit by the flames in the grey gloom. But get them as models you cannot, if it is a good olive year. No, the olives are fallen—they must be gathered. This is, I gather, a natural law, and cannot be broken.

The men take a heap of soft woven circular baskets,

which open out to the shape of a goldfish bowl ; they half fill them from the crushed mass on the mill bed, pile them neatly in one of the rugged wooden presses, and, taking a long wooden lever, begin to screw. If the weather is at all chilly boiling water is first poured over the baskets to help out the oil, and all this moisture runs down into a circular stone gutter and round to the mouth of a great stone tank underground, where it is left to settle.

As the pressure gets stiffer the two men fasten a rope to the end of their long lever from a thick upright pole fitted with a breast-high cross-piece ; and to this primitive windlass, in the half-lit arched extremity of the long building, they give their whole weight, and produce the best picture of the magazine series.

To continue the story of the oil :—from the first tank underground it is skimmed to other tanks—solid stone tanks standing round the walls and suitable for forty thieves—and there it again stays to settle and get rid of more impurities ; while the almost black, madder-coloured refuse of acid water is run off by wayside, field or watercourse, where its pungent smell and the scorched herbage of its course are characteristics of all the countryside.

After several settlings the oil is put into casks or skins and sent to market and export. A cart full of oil-skins is one of the few unpleasant sights of Corfu, for they stick up all leggily and shining, and the smell of the oil thus in bulk is nauseating.

The Olive Workers

It is very usual for proprietors to let out the season's oil crop to some peasant, who undertakes the whole working of the fruit and receives half the oil in return. This plan has obvious advantages, as it ensures the utmost results from the crop, and that the proprietor's olives will not be neglected because the overseer has fruit of his own to grind. For the Corfiote peasants are still in the childlike and primitive stage when constant supervision is desirable, and would hardly consider an engagement binding if it were to their own hindrance.

I am assured I may give my purse to a peasant to carry from end to end of the island. They are honest to their code, though eastern enough to love a bargain, but in small matters their code is similar to that of an English schoolboy in regard to his neighbour's apples. It is necessary to guard carefully all household supplies, such as sugar, coffee, vegetables, fruit, etc., or a rapidly increasing leakage sets in. The poorer peasants, who sell all their own little crops of fruit and vegetables, all luxuries like eggs and cheese, do not object to sweeten their diet of bread and oil by helping themselves from their landlord's portion. This little mistake is made easier by the undefended wayside trees, unfenced plots, and general freedom of passage over the island.

In one very notable way their morality takes precedence to ours—they are remarkably abstemious. During a four months' stay I saw only one drunken man, and that was on a festa, and he lay limp across

73

the loaded sacks of the pack-saddle, while his pony proceeded sedately homewards. We hoped no impatient motor-car (for it was on the Gastouri road, during the Kaiser's visit) would disturb them : for not even the peasants keep any rule of the road, so one cannot expect their beasts to do so alone.

The Greeks drink their own light wines, and are not averse to a glass of Cognac ; but the singing in the wayside *bottege* is tuned in pleasant harmonies ; and even the townsfolk keep a delicate taste for water, and are able to recognise the different sources from which the little white hand-carts are supplied, which, covered with green boughs, hawk water through the streets.

When summer heats come and fruits ripen, the peasants build themselves huts, arbours, and tree platforms, where they sleep among the olives beside their crops, to ward off marauders, and especially dogs. One of these thieves will ruin a vineyard in a single night, so they are consequently shot at sight.

After the vintage all return to winter quarters in the old solidly built stone houses and huts of the hillside villages ; retired sites, at utmost distance from the myriad pirates of former days, and still a safe refuge from lowland fevers. Often the peasants go miles to work in their scattered fields and woods,—little properties complicated by giving and receiving of dowries. Though they do not work well for others, yet in their uninquiring traditional methods they labour hard for their own land, so that the present gardens of Corfu are not so far below those, fabulous and famous, of Alcinous, which bore fruit twice a year, and even all the year round. For in April come the strawberries, followed by a most luscious array of cherries—such cherries !—amber and white and red and black, translucent in their glossy perfection, and competing for favour with the perfect gold of the nespoles. * This most refreshing of fruit is very beautiful, clustered among its dark green foliage. The lower knots can be picked in passing from the trees just outside the courtyard gate, and in all the orchard places and among the vineyards they are the richest note of colour.

By the beginning of June the early figs are ripe, sweet as honey, and mulberries, almost bursting with their own juice, and quite colouring the trees with their abundance. Apricots follow, and plums, pears, apples, and tomatoes ; while before the August figs are done and the later pears ripe, the first grapes are ready. And the grapes continue till Christmas, when the first oranges begin the year again.

Vegetables grow with equal luxuriance. Cauliflowers and purple-faced brocoli, leeks (very popular done with mild red pepper sauce), and potatoes, not rivalling ours, though quite good. Sweet potatoes, beets, onions, varieties of wild asparagus and other green things from the woods, and a great variety of pumpkins, marrows, and cucumbers furnish forth the year.

Fresh cheeses, almost as soft and white as a blanc-

* Loquat.

mange, are made from sheep's milk, and a little
dairy in the town collects milk from the neighbouring
villages and provides reliable butter. There is a
macaroni factory somewhere, I know, but commerce
is not obtrusive, and the island is really entirely agricultural and pastoral, living on its olives and vines, and
on its sheep and goats. Cows, requiring I suppose
more capital, are not very common, but show traces
of breeding that are absent in the other domestic
animals; for ponies and horses are poor things, and
dogs—well, they are just dogs. From burly yellow
and pied watch-dogs, often savage and sometimes
starved, to the most repulsive little fragments shivering
about the wayside shops, no one could assign them to
any known species, or even guess at their ancestry.

CHAPTER III
Village Life

EXCEPT that the present generations of peasants are free from the unchecked extortions of their overlords, and no longer exposed to the raids of all varieties of pirates, which throughout the ages have infested the shores of Greece, their life seems essentially unchanged since mediæval times.

As the village priests, indeed nearly all the clergy of the Orthodox Church, are of the peasant class, and most of the landlords are absentees, there is no outward stimulus to thought and progress; and it is only an exceptional peasant who goes beyond his bit of land and the thoughts of his fathers. So the laborious primitiveness of their agriculture, their methods of working field, olive and vine, are as unchanged as their ancestral faith and thoughts.

Outside the district of their own village, with its few miles of property and scattered hamlets, they have few interests. A woman who weds beyond these limits is almost considered to have made a foreign marriage, so separate are the village communities.

As a consequence, each district still keeps the ancient distinction of its women's costumes and head-dressing, though the men, less straitly tied to home, are adopting ordinary European clothes, and quite disturbing the picture.

An Artist in Corfu

So little have they really outgrown old habits though, that they still appear to have the ingrained habit of fear, the instinct of the small and conquered nation, which prompts to prevarication, feigned stupidity or untruth, when a question is asked or order given : to find some means of gaining time or escaping.

One can hardly otherwise account for their quite unreasoning and aimless perversions—puzzling by their very superfluity. Unless, like their pilfering of small edibles, etc., they are just a primitive people's surviving touch of childhood, and rather a lack of development than an active fault. Certainly one finds it easier to condone these failings in them than in one's own kind.

This primitiveness of the peasant, though partly caused by the absence of landlords and educated leaders, whose small shares of interest in the much divided properties rarely induce them to live outside the town, is also reactionary in its effects, for it makes a " civilised " life in the country almost impossible. Town servants cannot be induced to leave the walls, to which they are rooted as firmly as the peasant to his village, so country dwellers have to rely altogether upon the peasants' help, and that is a disturbingly uncertain quantity both in and out of doors.

First on settling in the country comes the difficulty of collecting a household. Possibly an old and un-attached man can be bribed out as cook, but the raw material of the peasant must provide maidservants.

The town servants are curious enough, from the

The Servant Question

English standpoint—averaging the appearance of a charwoman, very occasionally rising to cap and apron, more often falling beyond our English conception of slaveydom; but the country product is even quainter.

Delightful in appearance, of course, clean and neat in the pretty country costume, the peasant girl comes to try her hand at indoor work. Probably from an earth-floored hut, where she has hardly in her life seen the most ordinary fittings of a house. For days she is laboriously shown the uses of things, initiated into the mysteries of the dinner table, with its luxuriance of knives and forks, and ritual of serving. Then one morning it is announced that she has gone—just gone—been bored with the strange and unmeaning indoor tasks, and found the plentiful food and light work a poor substitute for the freedom and hard fare of her village home. So a new Sofia—it was generally Sofia—has to be sought and the same process repeated with her.

Once, in a Golden Age, there was Nina—who was a treasure. She quickly learned all her own work, and also how to manage and superintend old Dimitri, the cook, thus giving the administration a much-needed rest. She learned Italian also, very prettily she spoke, and charmed all visitors with her manners. Add to her virtues that she *took* nothing but coffee, that she cleaned the bicycles, and mended their punctures. This Paragon stayed two years, and there was peace in the land, and her delightful stitchery adorned E.'s blouses. Then—Nina went home to the village;

79

said, I think, that her mother wanted her to pick
olives (she was generally met water-carrying for the
palace alterations; no doubt it was quite interesting,
so many strange workmen, such opportunities for seeing
and hearing things), and when I arrived the two maids
whom she had trained were also leaving. Lisavé, the
handsome indoor maid, shortly departed—quantities
of oranges, onions, and other household stores vanishing
at the same time; while Sofia I., the carrier of water,
tender of sheep and donkey—in fact, hardly considered
an upstairs person at all—had to be our standby during
a long series, who came, raw from the village, or in-
capable and dreadful from the town, and invariably
vanished after a few days. Six of them within six
weeks was the record. One most strapping maiden
departed after a single night, for she did not like sleeping
alone, and others did not even excuse themselves.
The prize and model of the girls' orphanage, highly
recommended, was one of the experiments; aged 17,
she wept ceaselessly for two days, while all the household showered bribes and attentions; then she ran
away back to the orphanage, with her whole wardrobe
on her back—six miles, and getting on to hot weather.

The series included Katarina, from town, who was
not quite so untrainable as the rest, but whose sole
visible garment, for all occasions, was a black muslin
dress, *sans* collar, *sans* everything, and with the more
alarming of its rents pinned together. She went in
stockinged feet, too, till her father brought her a pair

of particularly gorgeous carpet slippers (she was in mourning). In the moist heat of early summer or on those spring days when sirocco tests the nerves, these minor troubles of life are trying and one understands why country life is not popular in Corfu.

The country marketing is as uncertain as the country household. A weekly donkey-load was brought every Sunday by Georgi, a bright young peasant from a neighbouring estate, who went into town and fulfilled his commissions with considerable discrimination, though I regret to say it was necessary to weigh and measure every item of the load, or, like the pitman's sovereign, it "wad hev pined" on the way. For the rest of the week we were dependent on local supplies. The village supplied bread and kid; beyond that we had what the peasants chose to bring. One day several women might have promised greenstuff, but there would be no vegetable for dinner; or we had met a fisherman. who volunteered to bring fish, but there would be no fish on the table : perhaps he changed his mind—who knows. Peasants who supply eggs do so at their own convenience; no eggs for us while Kaiser and Court offer a better market; eggs dumped on us by the dozen when it suits their vendors.

There was *always* maccaroni, of course, and Dimitri cooked all the southern dishes excellently—the vegetables quite a revelation even to a vegetarian; for we cannot afford here to eat globe artichokes the size of walnuts, shell and stalk and all ; nor indulge in marrows as small as a finger, brought to market with all the golden glory of their flowers ;—still a lot was due to Dimitri.

The Kaiser's holiday not only caused fluctuations in our egg market, but indirectly put a stop to " jamming " operations. Cherries and strawberries were ripe, but there was no sugar !

Little Corfu had so bestirred herself with *gendarmerie* and all precautions for the safety of her distinguished visitor that the accustomed supply of duty-free sugar, etc., was perforce temporarily cut off, and of course no one would think of buying expensive duty-paid sugar for preserving. So we had to wait.

I was told about one sack in a hundred might pay the almost prohibitive duty. But the other is the more usual way of entry.

The general method of procedure would begin with the advent of a small child with some sample tied in a cloth. Some of this beet sugar seems to have no sweetness at all ; but if up to requirements negotiations as to price would follow. One of the partners in the " run " would then appear and bargain, and in the evening the goods would be delivered.

Occasionally the affair did not end at this point. In a day or two another man might appear, demanding his share of payment, with accusations of partner's dishonesty. Nothing stereotyped about such housekeeping !

The Habit of Smuggling

Passing down the village street there would be a murmur, " Do you want coffee ?" replied to by remarks on weather and crops or other innocent subjects, after which a bargain might be unobtrusively struck and time of delivery appointed.

E. once said, " But how can you bring the petroleum this afternoon ? " and was answered, " The police have been paid to go to the village dance. It is quite safe."

Indeed, in a country poor as Corfu, with ruinous duties, accommodating shores, and the free-trade coast of Turkey so very handy, smuggling is inevitable, and is almost openly practised.

I remember one evening we were enjoying the usual sunset stroll (we " collected sunsets " so to speak), when a man running through the brushwood started Benjie, E.'s big peasant dog, barking violently. Presently, behind this scout, in proper adventure-book fashion, came a line of men, bent each under a heavy case, and making very good way over the rough ground and among the scrub. It was barely dark, and many of the homeward-faring peasants must have seen them before they had zigzagged steeply up from the shore and crossed the uneven open ground above, to gain the little gorge, where presumably they would wait till dark. But as this was the arrival of the village supply of petroleum, and as every one would buy it, there were none to condemn its somewhat shady arrival.

Our village of Gastouri lies about six miles south of

the town. It is one of the largest and most affluent, and lies high on the landward slopes of Sta. Kyria Ki, which is that charming little peaked crag, from the shoulder of which the Achilleion palace (built and beloved by the unfortunate Empress Stephanie) looks over the Straits and rolling olive-covered land. The village hangs irregularly about what is almost a ravine for steepness. Its road curls intricately among the scattered houses of light-coloured plaster and red tiles, and it is set in feathery olive and adornment of golden orange-trees and light sprays of blossom. The village properties extend for some miles north and south, and Gastouri can afford to hire from less prosperous districts bands of olive-pickers, and of young men to till its vines.

Its priests are kept busy with the three or four village churches, and the half-dozen isolated chapels which each have their special festas, and in some cases require quite a strenuous pilgrimage. On the summit crags of Sta. Kyria Ki there is not even room to get a sketch beside the tiny chapel and its sentinel cypresses, and it is reached by the steepest and roughest track, but on Easter Eve even the most ancient priests and all go up in procession, somehow.

Just over the waves, a mile or more away, is a fisherman's shrine, Sta. Sofia. It is hardly more than a tiny cave in the cliffside ; dark, till a match shows the faded wreaths and spent candles of some long past festa, and the decaying panels of the painted screen which divides even this minutest of Greek churches. One has to scramble down steeply to reach it, and step respectfully across its approach of very shaky and disintegrating boards, which show wave and stone through their gaps. It seemed a forgotten and melancholy little place.

Service in the village churches is popular, perhaps as much for its social as religious side, for the service of the Orthodox Church is still rendered in mediæval Greek—incomprehensible to many of the populace.

Some endurance is required in the worshippers, for Sunday and festa services last an hour or two, and there are no seats in the churches. I know at one service which the household was particularly anxious to attend, twenty-four hymns to the Virgin were to be included. There are little services at odd times in the week also, for often a bell is tinkling from one of the queer little belfries which stands each beside and detached from its church.

That the peasants' mediæval faith is still quite a reality is proved by a recent incident on my friends' estate. A vine-worker, having a grudge against the overseer, maliciously tore up the young sprouting vines and cast them wasted on the roadway. Now this was a very serious matter, going beyond personalities or pilferings, for if it were not checked, who in unwalled Corfu would be safe ? So the village stirred, and the priests took counsel together. Then, in church, they solemnly cursed the unknown thief. And this being an affair of grave import, the Metropolitan also gave his services and pronounced an arch curse in the Cathedral of Corfu. So the ravages were effectually stopped ; though the effect on ravager is not reported.

The oldest of the village priests is eighty-two, and he has served in Gastouri for fifty-two years. By a sensible rule, ordination does not take place till the age of thirty, and though one sees small boys of twelve in the costume of the priests' schools they are quite free to remain laymen when their education is finished, and free to marry before they take orders, though not afterwards, nor do they make bishops of the married clergy.

The Greek Church does not look with much favour on converts, theorising that, abandoning their old faith, they will not keep to any new. Nor does it like innovations, for when Queen Olga caused the Scriptures to be translated into the vulgar tongue, for the people's weal as she naturally thought, the deed seemed so sacrilegious that there were riots and burnings of the offending books in the streets of Athens. But there feeling runs so strong between the supporters of " pure Greek " and " popular Greek " that so rare an opportunity for action could hardly have been missed.

The Gastouri women are famous beauties, and their dress also is unexcelled in the island. On Sundays and festas they are magnificent, their superb bearing and grace carrying off the extraordinary richness of their costumes. They wear very full skirts, usually of black cloth, pleated, and with gay borderings of ribbon, but often of most brilliant shot silk ; and if the little apron is not also of silk, its muslin is covered with knots of ribbon, tinsel, spangles, lace, etc.

The pretty old fashion of their bodice, still seen in other parts of the island, left the full white sleeves showing, and was simply an open-fronted vest of some rich colour of velvet, thickly encrusted with gold embroidery, and fastened with two silver or gold buttons just above the girdle, which is generally of bright, vertically striped material of many colours. Now, the Gastouri belles have the fashion of wearing over this a short jacket, either of black cloth or coloured velvet, and it is as stiff as the vest with gold stitchery. On top of all this glitter are chains of gold and beads, and fine worked gold ornaments dangling over the white hand-worked chemise, and long slender bunches of gold drops hanging from ear to shoulder.

On the head a wonderful erection of hair is worked over a double series of cushions, to which it is bound with red ribbons. A fine muslin and lace-edged kerchief is turned back from the crown, and sometimes dotted with tinsel ornaments and coloured flowers. Brides, and those betrothed, are even more elaborately *coiffées*, for their muslin veils are stiffened to nearly a foot in height, and freely sprinkled with flecks of gold and colour, while over the rolls of hair is placed a great wreath of bright artificial flowers, ribbons,— mostly in primary colours of course,—tinsel, and so on. Imagine a group of these gorgeous beings passing along the village road with beautiful swinging walk, to cluster round the well.   They move perfectly, greet one with gentle voice, and a bow like a duchess.

On all the chief Sundays and on festas, there is a dance in any part of the village street that is not too steep ;   to its roughness the nimble-footed Greek seems indifferent.   The colour is hemmed in by irregular buildings, from walls, windows and stairways of which gorgeous heads look down (I wonder if it was the Crusaders who brought these Plantagenet-like coiffures north with them), while other spectators, keenly interested and critical, surround and take turns in the circle of the dance.

Under the stone arcade of a bottega, fiddler and mandolinist play away at their simple melodies, and a visitor is most courteously given a chair in the best place.   The dancing is kept up for hours, and if in honour of a bride, she is expected to dance all the time. The men, whose part is more exacting, frequently take rests and change places.

These dances have descended from the ancient *Romaika*.   The woman's part in them is always quite unchanging.   United in double or quadruple procession by their gay handkerchiefs, in a species of solemn two-step, they circle the village street ; a rhythmic bow of colour, within which the men execute their vigorous and intricate steps.   There is always one special leader of the dance, and no other man may take his place without offence.   He begins alone with the women, gathering the front row of handkerchiefs in his hand and moving backwards in front of them. At first his steps are hardly more than posturings, but as they get more animated, he drops the handkerchiefs, turns round, and with arms akimbo or raised begins a series of reel or hornpipe-like steps, while other men gradually join in, till there are half a dozen or so, shuffling and bounding, generally gracefully, within the circle. And always the women move round with unchanging rhythm and eyes demurely dropped, while behind them little barefoot children join in unchecked.

It is pictorially very regrettable that the younger men are abandoning the quaint island costume with its full blue *fustanella* knickers, and embroidered sleeveless coat and are adopting ordinary " ready mades " and sailor hats. The latter are particularly unfortunate for the picturesqueness of the dances : worn at very rakish angles, they generally fall off at the most dramatic moment ! There are still enough of the blue *fustanellas* among the older men to show what is lost by the change of costume. However, they *do* wear red scarves at the waist still.

For entertainment other than dancing Gastouri has a little theatre, where plays are performed by the young men of the village. But, doubtless from its neighbourhood to the imperial palace, Gastouri is really quite an advanced village, as things go, and I have not heard of any other such place of entertainment outside the town.

Sunday dances, an occasional visit to town for fair

or festa, a bridal—these are the country relaxations. For the rest of their lives the men hoe and plant or fish, the women weed and gather all day long, with a sleep in some tree-shaded spot after the simple dinner of bread and oil, and an exchange of news at the well in the evening.

I doubt that the women are always too hard at work in the fields to have developed many housewifely arts. Their neat hands make wonderful patterns and smockings on their chemisettes, though, and the art of patching is much developed. I have seen old dames with jackets so intricately and variously patched that none might say if original garment were there at all, and the full blue cotton skirts of everyday wear are generally varied in gentle degrees of faded patch.

But even those *poveri* who are beyond the needle's help, draped in Rackham-like festoons of rags, have some freedom or charm with them which stops short of English hopelessness of squalor.

The little tradesmen of the villages seem fairly prosperous, and some few villagers rise to affluence. In Gastouri there is portly Pei Petti, who created a village after his name, just down at the foot of the hills, whereof he is presumably landlord. He has a son M.P. in Athens, and of course there is much virtue in a tame M.P., for he can get roads and things for the district. So Pei Petti is Mayor of Gastouri and in that capacity presented a bouquet and address on the arrival of the Kaiser. Unfortunately it was a very

Cipi, the Albanian

muddy day, and portly Pei Petti slipped and the bouquet fell in the mud, for all the world to see.

It may shock you to learn that Corfu is still in that primitive attitude of mind which deems it fitting that the men beat their womenkind. E. says it is such a pity there is no one to beat the men too—the women work so much better.

Cipi, the overseer, only followed the custom in beating his wife; but it was not reasonable that he beat her for presenting him with a girl instead of the hoped-for boy baby, and that he continued to beat and blame when a second and third daughter arrived. Poetic justice has now been executed on Cipi, however, for a son was born to him at last, and now he is grown up and beats Cipi.

Cipi is really an Albanian; his father fled to Corfu after killing four Turks: unable to return, the exile established a monthly communication with his family by signal fires over the Straits, and lived in peace. They say he was a fine man, and probably the Turks needed killing. It is strange to meet people whose own grandmothers, no further back, were kept hidden in cellars all their youth for fear of the Turks. And it may account for much of the timidity of Corfiote women.

One of the daughters of Cipi became E.'s handmaid. Perhaps the parental beatings had not suited her; for she was ugly and very dull, and could not even learn how to use a door handle instead of the accustomed cottage latch, so very shortly she was dismissed.

An Artist in Corfu

Then a suitable husband was selected for her by the family; but she refused to marry him—begged and wept, till—this is a primitive tale—her brother beat her into the betrothal, which was duly announced. There was of course an absent lover; he returned from his term of conscription then, and coming to Maria at work in the fields he gave her bitter reproaches. "You knew that I loved you, and would marry you," said he. "Aye, but what could I do since you had not asked for me?" And that was true enough, for a modest maid is not supposed even to look at the men too much, and must say nothing over bold. So the man said, "Will you now break the betrothal and marry me?" And that was a bold enough proposal. So she must have thought of all the beatings, and her unloved betrothed; and the young life that so demands happiness made her answer, "My brother is making me a pair of shoes for the wedding, and they will be finished on Saturday. Then I will run away with you and we will be married."

So on Saturday, when her new shoes were made, Maria came to him in the woods, and they went away and were married in defiance of the brother, and the beatings, and the betrothed. And I think Maria must have been happy, for she became smiling and beautiful, and no longer too stupid to know how a door opens. But alas, they did not live happily for ever after, for, whether it was the parental beatings or the barbarous advice of village wives, she became very ill,

Maria

and after a useless visit to the hospital at Athens, died, lingering, in her woodland home over the Straits, where she had been used to smile pleasantly on us from her upper window as we passed.

CHAPTER IV

The Way to Town

THERE are two ways from Gastouri. Except in summer heat the most enjoyable and lovely is by the donkey track along the coast ridge, through olive woods overhanging the Straits, to the ferry at the mouth of the lagoon. It is a winding two miles of absolute beauty. The grey-green harmonies of the olives are never without some touch of pleasant colour; all through the spring they enshrine the beauties of the blossoms; and ever they frame wonderful glimpses of Straits and mountains. There are little orange orchards nestled in the denes, and tiny patches of tobacco, and queer huts of stone or reeds that one expects to meet only in an adventure-book, and there is shade nearly all the way.

Down at the mouth of the lagoon are two charming islets. The Pontikonisi, or mouse island, sometimes called the isle of Ulysses; and the even tinier islet of Nuns. The former is an abrupt little rock, clad with cypresses and crowned with a tiny chapel. It bears a strong resemblance to Böcklin's "Isle of the Dead." The Nuns' Island is at sea-level, often wave-washed, and just large enough to support the simple white-washed building of a little nunnery;—a complete and sunny contrast to the crags and dark cypresses of its

94

WINTER DAY ON THE LAGOON.

fellow. A little broken causeway nominally connects the Nuns' islet with the northern shore of the lagoon.

About a mile along the southern shore to our left is the clear running stream of Cressida, and peasants say that it was here that Nausicaa and her maidens had been washing linen, by the old legendary city on the shore of the lagoon, when they found Ulysses cast ashore.

Arrived at the ferry we must yell very loud for Spiro, if there is no peasant also waiting to do it for us. He generally comes, in time, when his interest in fishing is not too keen, and ferries us over in a large fishy tub, with octopi and pinnæ and such curios lying about. The northern lip of the lagoon rises quite abruptly from the shore, and on the summit is the site of One Gun Battery, or Canone, as it is now called. There is a café on top, and as it is usually the first show place to which tourists are brought, the road from here to town is haunted by little rogues of children with flowers or oranges, running beside the carriages to beg " pendarras." Except for them it is a very pleasant road. From the Canone the views inland over the lagoon are beautiful. Olives and orange gardens hide the few villas built on this favoured spot, and by climbing the higher ground between the road and the sea a foot-passenger can easily get up to Ascensione,* a tiny village and church, where the great panegyric of the Ascension festa is held. This is supposed to be the site of the oldest town in Corfu, Palæopolis, and near at hand are

* Greek Analipsis.

the only remaining fragments of ancient buildings in the island.* The ruins of a small Doric temple, possibly to Neptune, were discovered here in 1822 by a British officer.

The ancient town was sacked by the Goths in the sixth century, and during the middle ages much of the ancient masonry was used for strengthening the defences of the town as occasion required. So though there were stores of marble there so late as the seventeenth century, Corfu is now left with hardly a trace of her ancient people.

A short mile to the north of Ascensione is Mon Repos, a small country villa built by a British Governor, General Adams, and now belonging to the King of Greece. The villa stands well over the sea, and from its terraces there are exquisite views over the widest expanse of the Straits, and over Kastrades Bay (the ancient Garitza) to the town and outstanding forts and their background of mountains. The grounds are usually open to the public, and are very charming in a half-wild way, with trees and flowering shrubs, jutting crags, and reedy dips to the sea.

Tucked away beside the gate of Mon Repos is the tiny convent of St. Euphemia ; and from the rock just in front of it is the finest view over Kastrades—the great sweep of the bay ending in the long bold line of

---

* At the pretty fishing village of Benizza, six miles to the south, there are the remains of a Roman bath with mosaics in one the orange orchards ; and nearer the town is the tomb of Menekrates beside the new museum.

A Byzantine Church

the forts. Just below, the suburbs begin, and here to the right of our road is the picturesque outline of the oldest church in the island; a most charming pile of Byzantine work, dedicated to Saints Jason and Sosipetro, saints who were companions of St. Paul and are said to have been the first Christian preachers in Corfu. In this little church are incorporated remains of heathen temples, two pillars of grey marble being a welcome change from the usual paint and plaster of Corfiote churches. It is the only Byzantine church in the island, and probably dates from the twelfth century.

Shortly after passing the church the road emerges from this corner of suburbs upon the broad marina, which embraces the whole wide curve of the bay. This is infinitely the finest approach to the town, with all the glories of the Straits on the right, and the forts in front. I can strongly recommend it for sunsets. It is always regrettable when hot weather stops this delightful walk to town and one must cycle the dusty road, or endure a village carozza, to get there.

But the main road is not without its interests. For the novice from England even the descent of the Gastouri hill is an experience. There is not much *driving* in Corfu. The horses manage all that themselves, loose-reined; the man on the box does a violent bit of steering on occasion, and uses his whip and the motor-horn when necessary to clear the road of peasants. The vehicle goes swinging round the sharp and badly surfaced zig-zags at a good swift downhill trot, and by the wisdom of the horses comes to no grief. One meets the town carriages returning thus in the evening without lamps. Many corners are unwalled or have deep drops into vineyards.

Of course, this soon ceases to be remarkable or exciting, but the infinite variety of the road traffic is not staled by custom, and I always enjoyed the drive thoroughly.

From the foot of the hill we are on the " grand trunk road " of the southern half of the island, and it is full of pictures. There are bevies of peasant women going to work, or to market with the fruits of the season on their heads ; or later, laden with autumn gleanings of fodder and firewood. These are pleasant family groups—the donkey's wide load making a capital lounge for the baby ;—a black-robed priest on a narrow white horse, all adorned with his week's marketing of cotton bundles and coloured sacks and leeks and crockery ;—an old man draped in multitudinous blue rags, tending a red cow by the wayside ;— a colony of nomad Albanians on hire for the olive harvest, their beds on the backs of the neat little women, the men with hoe on shoulder and lordly in enormous shaggy cloaks. There were always beautiful colour and movement, and a fascinating variety of costume, and often some funny incident of traffic or accident to be noted.

Nearer town there would be great herds of milk-goats coming out from their daily pilgrimage of the streets; and little pyramids of cauliflowers and turnips brought from adjoining market gardens for sale by the roadside, and primitive *bottege*, seemingly the meeting places for animals as much as men. Donkeys, cows, goats and fowls collected round the rude table of one especially—a proper club for them it seemed.

It was useless to try and hurry along this road, except in the empty hours of early afternoon, for peasants and their charges are not to be hastened; they have, moreover, no rule of the road, and slowly change their mind in the middle. They think a bicycle can stand still as easily as a donkey, and a bicycle bell never has any effect on primitive people. In Corfu one must shout " Bross, am *Bross !* " with great vigour, and then they consider a move, though probably leaving their donkey broadside on. Goats are the only things that always make way.

In springtime the blossom is wonderful in the flat meadows about the lagoon, where the market gardens are; ditches, not fences, divide the land, so the view is not broken, and the peach-trees vanish into a cloud-like distance of pink, backed by the blue line of Albanian hills. In the late autumn large herds of goats and flocks of turkeys are led among the vineyards to fatten for the winter festas. Such delightful scarecrows are some of their drovers! And on the wide marshy meadows where the English made a racecourse there are generally some Albanian shepherds with their flocks—fine primitive pastoral figures. From this point there are two ways to town : straight on is the back way, intricate with goats and children and small shops and stalls ; the other is round to the right by the Albanian village, and so on to the marina.

Whether from persecution or crime many Albanians come over to live in Corfu, and there is quite a large colony here. The Albanians are probably descendants of the ancient Illyrians, and are fine soldiers. They prefer pastoral to agricultural life, and opposite Corfu their hills are burnt bare for pasturage. The men are strong highland-looking fellows and have a fine costume too. They wear either the full white *fustanella* (kilt), or long breeches of thick felt-like cloth fitting gaiter-wise from knee to foot, ornamented with braided patterns at seams and waist. They all have wide scarves or leather belts stuck thick with implements and weapons, and over their sleeveless vests of black or white (matching the breeches) wear a covetable variety of blanket coat or cloak, usually in white or grey cloth, that might be a blanket made of goat's hair. Some of these coats fit smartly to the waist, with slashed and braided sleeves, and very full and short kilted skirts, while others are more in full cloak form, with a hood, and braided sleeves buttoned back. Yet another variety has long hair, so that it seems like a matted sheepskin, but is really a manufactured material. They wear the tarbush, but would prefer to be Greek subjects, as they consider themselves Greeks. Doubtless many have good reasons for not returning to Albania.

The Albanian

The Albanian women are rather small, not amply built like the women of Corfu, nor beautiful as a rule. They have a very neat costume of dark blue cloth; the skirt is short and fully gathered from a wide band fitting right down on to the hips, and this adds to the small and girlish appearance of their figures. They carry burdens on their shoulders, not their heads, so have not the fine carriage of our islanders. They wear a queer little cap or tiara, usually of black and white, and partly composed of turban twists. It seems remarkably liable to disarrangement, and is often at the rakish angle of a Glengarry bonnet. But for festas it is more tiara-like, and stiff with silver and stitching.

Though warriors immemorially, the Albanians became as peaceful, in Corfu, as any other inhabitant of an island where serious crime is rare. They follow the avocations of peace in town and country, their picturesque groups adorn the cafés about the harbour, and doubtless they smuggle as guilelessly as the natives. One of them, a witness in a law court, when asked his trade or profession, answered calmly, " Contraband."

CHAPTER V
The Kaiser's Holiday

BY the beginning of April Corfu was all astir to welcome her exalted visitor. Not only did Athens send beautiful mounted guards to ride up and down the roads, with more beautiful officers to see they did it, but for some weeks preceding the arrival of the Kaiser foot soldiers appeared like mushrooms all over the place, and extra guards made the usual easy smuggling impossible. Those men must have inventoried every olive in the district, I think, and during the imperial visit our comings and goings were quite strictly noted.

Such a responsibility is a Kaiser that the roadside hedge of prickly pear, an ancient and massive growth along the road to town, was all laid bare and open; and there was a kind of curfew regulation for the closing at ten o'clock of all cafés in town, which fell rather hardly on a population accustomed to sit late after the heat of the day.

Personally, in Gastouri, we only felt the closing of a right of way through the narrow slip of hillside (it is called in German The Park) connecting the palace with the shore. We were now cut off from some of our most delightful rambles southward along the coast, and the fishers of Benizza, whose way to town had been left open under the Austrian ownership, were obliged to leave their woodland track for a long steep detour by the village road. For now gates and high iron wire, and a guard of twenty-two gendarmes took the place of a perfunctory hedge which before had marked the boundaries.

With many imported workmen, Gastouri had been busy making an artesian well, repairing the palace, and building a large and strikingly plain annexe down the landward side of the hill. Never had easy-going Corfu so hastened to get things finished in time, and we wondered if the annexe-d portion of the suite caught many colds.

As the Kaiser approached, the atmosphere began to hum with rumour, and continued to do so until the Imperial presence was withdrawn. Some rumours were serious and some were comic, some were credible and some were wild—that King Edward must also have a palace in Corfu, since he could not be outdone by the Kaiser ; he was going to have it over in the west by San T'odera, and Queen Alexandra too ; she had bought Pelleka, that charming little coned hill with the villages—King George was at last going to receive his long-neglected Corfiote subjects, and then there would be a ball, and so on—rumours of spies too, and of precautions against them.

King George of Greece, the Crown Prince and Princess, with other members of the royal house, were in residence, and the little town made gay and pretty preparations for the Kaiser's arrival; while all the peasants flocked to greet first their King and then their visitor. The landing stairs were richly decorated in Oriental style, and the whole front of the esplanade was arcaded with rose wreaths and greenery of very charming design by Mr. Giallina.

Now was it not sad, when everything in the island was so determinedly gay, that the weather should be so sulky! Heavy clouds, with drenching rain, swept the island for days beforehand, and on the eve of the arrival culminated in a thunderstorm accompanied by hail. Luckily the paper roses were weather-proof, but the festa costumes of the waiting crowds must have suffered, and only a short lull allowed the imperial motors time to reach the Achilleion, after the family and official welcomes in town.

We had seen the *Hohenzollern* pass close under us in the morning; a fierce and business-like man of war very close behind, and both steaming most strenuously. A great thundering of guns soon after announced their arrival.

Old Dimitri, who was prevented from any further sight-seeing by the weather, went about in deep childish disappointment, muttering, " If the weather were a man I would kill him, I would kill him." While Sokrate, the village idiot, was overheard to remark more philosophically to the heavens, " Aye, Rain, rain then! It is your right."

So it rained, and the illuminations and fireworks

were delayed for days ; and when the village assembled
at the Achilleion gates, fat Pei Petti slipped in the mud
and dropped his bouquet and his dignity together
before the imperial motor, and Corfu's charms were
lost in mist and mud.

Gastouri was, of course, particularly interested in
the visitors : more intimately interested, so to speak ;
for the village men had been working in palace and
grounds, and the maidens carrying water and materials
there, and the householders storing furniture and
effects. Also Gastouri knew from experience the
commercial value of a Court in residence. The village
welcome was pretty to see even under the grey skies,
and the new arrivals seemed to think so too. Princess
Louise looked particularly interested in all that passed.

Warships of several nationalities, English, Austrian
and Greek, had come into Corfu's beautiful bay to
greet the Kaiser, and with these he was much occupied
during the first days of his visit. The first morning
he visited each in turn in correct uniform as admiral,
with quick changes between on the *Hohenzollern*. The
thunder of their salutes as he boarded and left each
vessel was constantly awaking the island, and we
thought the imperial holidays were to be indeed
strenuous. However, the island peace soon returned,
warships steamed away, and the Kaiser with his family
spent their days in long motor tours, or walking among
the olive woods and fields of the near country.

In company of a numerous suite, and with flying

squadrons, so to speak, of gendarmes in advance among the vineyards, the first imperial walk was attempted. (History does not report what courtly feet suffered from the unaccustomed rocky paths.) But in a few days the Kaiser and his consort were wandering practically alone through the woods and by the cottages and orchards, in friendly acquaintanceship with the peasants, and doubtless rejoicing in the simple courtesy which made such freedom possible.

The Kaiserin, with Princess Louise, often walked in the village at evening, invariably carrying a hand camera, and always finding use for it among the groups of women about the well, and family parties returning from work. The Kaiserin always wore simple dresses of walking length, so the often alarming steepness of the woodland paths and short cuts never checked her explorations.

The Achilleion is really almost a mountain home. Built high on the northern shoulder of Sta. Kyria Ki, it commands unsurpassed views over land and Straits, and is itself a gleaming white landmark for half the island.

From its airy terraces nearly the whole extent of the Ionian Straits is visible to the east, while northward lie town and forts and a wonderful inlay of sea and mountain :—The beautiful bay of Govino, backed by the fine severe line of Spartile's cliffs and peaks which cuts across the north end of Corfu, and beyond this again the towering, shouldering ranges of Epiros,—the Acroceraunian mountains,—white for half the year.

THE VILLA ACHILLEION (WEST FRONT).

The Achilleion

To the west, the undulating olive-covered land is backed by little hills, from which Pelleka and S. Giorgio beyond it are distinguished by their striking form. The view is terminated by the great mass of Santi Deka, that mountain of beautiful mists and wonderful atmosphere, rising beyond the deep gorge of Gastouri.

The Achilleion Palace was built for the late Empress Elizabeth of Austria in 1890-91. It is in modern Renaissance style by Raffaelo Carito, of Naples, and the decorations are in imitation of Pompeii. It is really rather painful as a work of art. Internally there is no colour scheme ; externally the place looks a misfit. But its site is superb and the grounds are charming. Sta. Kyria Ki is too steep to accommodate its entire bulk at one level, so the sea front is two storeys above the main south door. At the higher level is a beautiful terrace of great palms, which commands almost the whole range of the views. The breeze is fresh under the rustle of fronds, and the sea never looks bluer than between their greenery ; cool ivied arcades flank it and flowers cover the ground. The statue of the dying Achilles (by Herter) gleams whitely in the midst. Less admirable sculpture adorns the adjoining terrace of the muses on the seafront of the palace, and some scenes from Greek story and song painted on the verandah walls are really very primitive indeed, somehow reminding one of the Sunday school illustrations of one's youth.

As one descends towards the shore the garden ceases

107

and the grounds are almost left to nature; the path zig-zags steeply through the shade of olives, almonds, oranges, lemons, oleander, syringa and all the easy growth of the island. There are a few patches of scarlet lilies and flowers of strong growth among the wilder vegetation, but mostly the beauties are Corfu's own : deep-toned cypresses, and rich colours of orange trees, and fairy lightness of blossom among the woods, and always the gleam of Albania's snows over the wonderful blue.

A statue of the late Empress of Austria now replaces that of a banished Heine in a little temple half-way to the sea, and a colossal triumphant Achilles has just been erected at the end of the terraces. Discreetly hidden in trees and grotto is the artesian well, which brings such an enviable gush of water for the palace use, and the pulse of which sends a throb of modernity through the mediæval atmosphere.

In a land where, at the end of summer, wine is cheaper than water, and where animals even die of drought in a bad year, it is indeed a happy Kaiser who can afford water in abundance even for his garden.

But the flowers which can endure unwatered give flower-lovers small reason for complaint in Corfu. Stocks, carnations, roses, mignonette, wallflowers, irises, sunflowers, chrysanthemums, peonies, all flourish with little care, and the wild flowers are quite un-countable. There is such a wealth of flowering trees, too, *all* the blossoms from almond, the first, to the last, quince. Splendid magnolias; syringas snowy with blossom; oleanders in masses of colour; acacias; the judas-tree's solid pink against the hills; flaming pomegranates dotted casually with nespolés and other fruit-trees among the vineyards. Really a set garden is a superfluity of beauty.

Over the Kaiser's land, as everywhere, springs the wild wealth of blossom. There is the scent of hidden violets under the trees, with a glimmer of anemone stars and irises; there are many of our English wildflowers beside stranger growths of pitcher plants and orchis, and there is an extraordinary variety of peas, vetches, and clovers.

Only on the summit terraces wild Corfu is banished, and there around the villa elaborate planning evokes a blaze of splendid colour during the imperial visit. Wistaria threads the marble balustrades, and scarlet anemones flame against them, carnations are much favoured, and there are carpets of the most beautiful tulips and pansies, and more oriental carpets of ranunculi and nemesia growing with eager and incredible profusion. There are stocks and roses and arum lilies and forget-me-nots, and in the strong light and shade of the palms there are great beds of cinerarias, each massed in tones of one colour only, and almost startling in the velvet richness of their blues, when one had in one's mind the sea distance as the very essence of colour.

During my second visit to Corfu a lucky chance enabled me to enjoy the best weeks of the garden.

An Artist in Corfu

Shortly before the Kaiser was expected I had received from Berlin my permission to paint in the Achilleion grounds. But I scarcely hoped to get what I wanted from it, for the flowers seem planned to open as the Kaiser arrives and to die when he departs, so I thought only buds and seed pods would be my portion.

However, only a few days before the expected arrival, and when the garden was all ready and waiting, Kaiser William's holiday was cancelled—I believe Parliament needed looking after, and it was not considered advisable to be so far from home—so I was left to enjoy undisturbed the whole cycle of the garden's unfolding in perfection of spring weather. I wish I could tell you what that atmosphere is really like. The flowers really look as though they enjoyed growing in Corfu more than anywhere else.

On the Kaiser's few yards of coast there is a tiny landing-place, just big enough for a boat or small launch, and beside it a bathing hut on piles, and an electric power station. Ignoring the last, the coast is very bonny here; there is that exquisite finish and gracious perfection of form which is always so satisfying in Corfu; and the Straits are always wonderful. Olives drop almost over the little lapping waves, their foliage spreads up to the fine crags of Kyria Ki. A mile or two to the south lies the little village of Benizza; on the shore below towering S. Stavro. Hardly to be distinguished in former years, and now only divided by a high wire fence, the small holdings of the peasants lie on either side the Kaiser's land, their owners working daily so close to this spirit of modern Europe, yet in life and thought at some century's remoteness.

Concerning the importance of Emperors, I think it was Cipi told us this story of Urania, who lives in a hut along the road by the oil magazine.

When the Kaiserin went for a walk she was usually accompanied by two little brown dachshunds, which marched in most soldierly discipline before her. One day, while we were away, E.'s great peasant dog Benjie, doubtless in need of exercise, accosted these retainers with his usual blundering friendliness. He probably looked very large and alarming, and there was a prompt rush of gendarmes armed with rock, and with the little swords which are drawn so readily on a dog. Whereupon Urania ran forth to Benjie's aid, crying, " Hold ! It is the dog of Count Dousmani." *And the Emperor was afraid then.* So Benjie did not die.

The Kaiser's brown motor-cars, matching the brown and gold of his liveries, and with pretty silver bugle calls, were soon well known on all the passable roads of the island. Taking into consideration the unsophisticated ways of the peasants, who take no notice of a bicycle call, and of their animals, which know no rule of the road, the entire absence of accidents was remarkable, especially when the mile-long hills and passes are considered, with their broken surfaces and alarming corners.

An Artist in Corfu

Corfu imported an Italian opera company for a special season when the Kaiser came. As every one has a box, and the repertoire is extremely limited, the entertainment is more of social than musical interest, though this little company gave some of the old favourites quite creditably.

It is a nice little theatre and several gala performances were given, and attended by King George of Greece and various members of the royal families. On these occasions the simple Corfiotes applauded at their own good pleasure, without waiting for the customary royal assent. This may have been in the nature of a hint to their King that they do not see enough of him to know better. Except for family parties and strictly official presentations, there was no royal entertaining. Doubtless the enormous German suite, totalling 150 I believe, reinforced by the smaller Greek suite, held a sufficiency of society. But Gastouri did its part of entertaining, for after much drilling the village school-children came to the gate of the Achilleion and sang the German national anthem. A little serenade which so pleased the Kaiser that he encored it.

The customary dances of the spring festas were being held in all the villages, and on a certain Sunday Gastouri was invited to send a selection of its best dancers up to the Achilleion. However, the village " masters of ceremonies " courteously but firmly declined ; firstly, because the absence of so many would spoil the dance for all the village, and more seriously because

The Departure of the Kaiser

the selection of the fairest dames was a task too risky and invidious for such near connections to undertake !

Variations of this story having swiftly flown about the town and district, with added rumours of the gifts which the Kaiser had intended distributing to the villagers on this occasion, a great assemblage of the curious flocked to Gastouri on the Sunday afternoon, carriage hire rose to truly imperial rates, and invading hordes cleared the village *bottegas* to their last crumb, and of course crowded out the native dancers. Naturally the Kaiser did not appear.

On the following Sunday he was to depart ; bidding farewell to Gastouri and going on board on Saturday afternoon. So when a great thundering of guns was heard on the Sunday morning, we concluded that was the end of his visit.

Late in the afternoon we strolled up to the village to watch the dancing as usual, and I had just settled comfortably to sketch when the familiar bugle call was heard, and dancers and spectators scattered in astonishment as the Kaiser's car swung swiftly up the street, its occupants in highest good humour at the joke of an unexpected return.

An officer in one of the following cars halted to invite all the villagers to dance at the Achilleion, and off they trooped at once, and danced for an hour or two, to the great pleasure of the Kaiser and his party, who were keenly interested. Some of the more imaginative peasants even said the imperial family took part in the

dance. At any rate the princess had a beautiful festa
dress embroidered, in preparation, it was said, for a
costume ball in Berlin.

There is no doubt the Kaiser and his family were
charmed with their Corfu holidays. He confirmed
the island's reputation by calling it a paradise, and
the island was equally charmed with him.

CHAPTER VI

Hot Weather

THEY told me I was the first Englishwoman to sleep in an olive-tree bed : if they knew, all the others would envy me. Corfu's heat is heavy, and when it became impossible to sleep comfortably indoors we invited Babadoni to make bowers.

The first year the old man was so busy that he made us one only ; so E. and I had to take turns for cool nights, but on my second visit we each had our own. No one but peasants had ever thought of sleeping in a bower before, which seems strange : and when our friends heard of it—only another example of English madness—there was a general chorus of alarm. We would get fever, also it was so unprotected. They really seemed almost to expect us to die of it in some way, and of course we ought to have been afraid of the vague things of the night. However, we were not, we enjoyed our bowers thoroughly and flourished in them.

Imagine ! Slipping out into the warm whispering dusk of a starry summer night, feeling one's way up the sloping trunk, to a bower of olive tree, wind-moved; where the breeze and stars come through the walls of green, and moonlight plays with the veil of olive leaves

12

above, and rosy dawn enters triumphant from over the Straits.

Babadoni is a very dear friend of mine, of an ancient and dignified order of peasants. All summer long he lives alone in a hut about half-way down to the sea ; and on Sundays and festas he comes to call, has a cup of coffee, or a Cognac and cake, sits and talks awhile on the vineyard wall or by the hammocks, then quietly does any odd jobs of tidying, pruning and such-like that he sees are needing him.

He delighted in making our bowers—*barraka* is the right term,—and did them very charmingly.

A suitable olive is the first necessity, one with firm trunks widespread about six or eight feet from the ground. On these a foundation of other trunks and branches is fixed, with support from a corner post or two in the earth, if necessary, and on these again a foot or two of green myrtle, broom, heath or any springy twigs from the ground around is carefully laid down. Here ends the simplest form of *barraka*. But ours were continued with tents or canopies of reeds and loose-woven twigs about the head for privacy, and completed by grass mats, on which our sheets were spread every evening. Rough steps, stuck in and on the trunk, led up, and as the beds faced the centre of the olive-tree they were reasonably screened from stray peasants taking short cuts.

I cannot describe to you the joy of being allowed the

freedom and space of the night, of feeling part of the wonderful out-of-doors.

The neighbours were partly right in thinking it unprotected. The first *barraka* was a good shout's distance from the house—beyond the nearest vineyard. I was the first to experiment, and it was decreed that Benjie, our quite adequate watch-dog, should be in charge. Benjie always began well, but with great regularity he shortly vanished, and after a time we found that old Dimitri, the cook, considered his hens less capable of self-defence than we, and tempting the dog back every evening, chained him by the hen house at the back-door.

However, we never needed a protector. The only thing that disturbed was an occasional thunder-storm, and once a snake, which took possession of E.'s bed, which she courteously gave up to it for the night.

Of course we could not but arise with the dawn. It seemed natural and inevitable, as I suppose it seems to the birds. Santi Deka * behind us made magic with golden and rosy mists about its crags, and we hastened to bathe before it was too hot.

We literally lived out of doors now, only going in to dress, and for midday heat when no outdoor shade seemed deep enough.

The hammocks hang just beyond the courtyard wall (it is rather an eastern courtyard, like the compounds of Madras it has an imposing barred iron gate in front,

* Άγιοι Δεκα.

and a large unfilled opening at the side), between four great olive trunks, and this summer drawing-room is roofed with a dense woven thatch of wistaria-green when the tasseled silken pavilion of spring has vanished. There are chairs, and a little unlocked green cupboard for cushions and work. The long lazy afternoons are spent there, half asleep in the heat ; and there, too, we sit till bedtime, with the tropic whirr of insects on the air, and fireflies weaving their busy little rhymes over the vineyards.

We dine out of course, on the east terrace, which is cool behind the house in the evenings, and over the Straits far below stray the wonderful colours of dusk and moonlit night.

About sunset time I used to go down seaward to the arcadian property of old Babadoni, and paint till dusk. Very hot that hill, even then, baked through by the morning sun. The dear old man was not always ready to sit for me, for he was exceedingly busy and active, in spite of his years, but I always found a little table and stool set ready for my work, and some arrangement of ripe nespolés or mulberries for my refreshment. He was quite proud of being painted, and now we correspond ; that is, I send him picture postcards, and he sends me messages by friends.

When I was leaving Corfu he came to bid farewell with a fragrant posy and a huge basket of lemons, such beauties. Deck passengers of course always carry their food, and it was a kind thought for hot weather

BABADONI AT HOME.

travelling. Our party enjoyed those lemons all the way home.

Babadoni had quite a considerable property scattered about in bits, and some very fertile patches, so his Sunday offerings of fruit were always delicious, and his sheltered garden seemed able to produce one or two carnations, roses or stocks for us on any day of the year.

Dimitri, the cook, was of quite a different caste to old Adoni (Babadoni—Papadoni—gaffer—daddy—Adoni). Dimitri is a townsman, a family relic who only followed his patrons into the despised country-house in extreme old age and incapacity. His mind is that of a child, and his appearance that of a vastly overblown and rather dilapidated cherub. Nature has decreed that he has usually a hole worn through the most prominent part of his apron, and he has a lisp complicated by the strong Venetian patois of the town.

It was occasionally my duty to wrestle with the household affairs, and it was one long exercise of patience. The most harassed and unfortunate housewife in England has no conception of the possibilities of accident, damage and mistake in Corfu, with peasants raw from fields and huts, and no well-stocked shops to mend matters.

Of course it was acknowledged that Dimitri's hens got far more than their fair share of the scraps, while the household dogs went often hungry, so one of our tasks was to extract from Dimitri enough bread for a decent meal. Every one eats bread in quantity in Corfu. Servants' allowance is 1 lb. a day each, and they often get more. While Dimitri was making his slow pilgrimage to the magazine for the daily allowance of charcoal—now becoming a very laborious business indeed for the old man—I would look in the biggest cooking-pot, search the disused oven, the cupboard, and other hiding holes, and generally managed to supplement the scanty " all there is, Signorina " from his secret hoards. But of course there was always the risk that I might be taking food lawfully belonging to a servant. For each takes his or her whole share of whatever is provided, and if they cannot finish then and there, some is put away till they can deal with it.

There was a certain rather terrible table drawer where these relics usually lurked, a mausoleum of dead dinners, and often I have been stopped from serving the dogs by a hasty claim from one or other of the servants.

Dimitri after a festa was ofttimes dreamy and unintelligible, and we were thankful when the dinner came up as it was meant. On one occasion he did send up a risotto with sugar as a sweet course, and he was capable of forgetting half the dinner. He was at his best on jamming days—hot mornings when cherries seemed interminably stony and strawberries ridiculously small. Then his only duty was to stir, and attend to the *fornella* (even that he would forget if not watched, —maddening for cake-making) ; so with time to spare

and one free hand he would relate legends of the saints
and of Corfu's history.

Dimitri was an artist in all the southern cookery,
but old age was hard upon him and his hand was no
longer sure. It was really time he was set aside to
moulder quietly away. But housekeeping is not easy
in Corfu, and he *could* cook very well.

His *capo d'opera* was mayonnaise sauce, which took
him a whole hour to make and was evidently one of
the higher mysteries of an initiate ; for he would often
tell of a very skilled cook of his acquaintance who once
spoiled *sixteen* eggs in making one mayonnaise !

Southern cookery has, I think, a finer finish than ours
as a rule. In those lands the lord of the kitchen is
not bothered by the et-cæteras of cakes and sweet things :
they are the department of the confectioner ; there
too he denies all knowledge of puddings, which are his
mistress's concern. So he simplifies his duties. But
within his own limits he is excellent. What northern
cook has old Dimitri's feeling and patience with a stew,
or his unrivalled touch in frying ? Though he is
verging on dotage, his instinct and training rarely fail ;
and with his pan hovering over a handful of charcoal
he exemplifies the artistic superiority of the genuine
craftsman over any modern combination of mechanism
and ingenuity.

Corfiote cookery favours the Italian, rather than
the Turkish taste of mainland Greece. Its maccaronis
and vegetable dishes are of excellent and never-ending

variety ; and E. tells of a certain temporary cook, who, from one piece of meat—by courtesy a steak—cooked a new and palatable dish for fourteen meals.

But that of course was not in hot weather.

In hot weather, milk, meat and any things perishable were all hung in a basket down a well—the only cool place. They had to be down a drinking-well, moreover, as other wells had no locks. Now there was a large serpent which also lived about that well, and one day he went down the rope, and the maids having too carelessly tied on a piece of meat, he dislodged it into the water, and no efforts could recover it. So through all the summer one of the best and nearest drinking wells had to be regrettably wasted on the garden, and laboriously purified at the end of the drought.

Corfu suffers very much from drought : there are few permanent rivers and springs, and presumably the scattered village populations have not capital enough to make storage from the winter rainfall, so they are often in sore straits if summer has been long and rains are late. Well after well is emptied, till the parched animals must be led for miles in search of a drink, and wine is cheaper than water. In really bad years the animals die, of course, and some villages are abandoned.

The rich herbage of Corfu is all burnt to a beautiful pale gold colour, as clear as lacquer, and the few head of stock from each peasant house are massed into large herds and led away by a shepherd to wherever water and pasturage can be found.

The Drought in Corfu

The woodlands are curiously still and empty after all the olives are gathered and the herds gone. The peasants go to their fields at early dawn, sleep in the shade at midday, and return late home ; or they live altogether in huts on their properties as soon as the earth is dug and fever gone from the lower lands.

About July Corfiotes consider it is warm enough to bathe, and that and boating are their chief recreations for the summer. A very few families migrate to their country homes for the hot weather, but most prefer to endure the town, where they become more and more nocturnal as the heat increases.

CHAPTER VII

Autumn

SUMMER passes with the first rain, due to arrive some time after the vintage, in October. But it is of no tropical regularity, and has been known even to precede the vintage work with a thorough drenching.

In 1909 the first rain came abnormally early: came up with a thunderstorm in the night, and burst at dawn, driving us indoors with hastily gathered bedding. Many times in that unusual season did we lie listening to a slow circling storm, risking it to the last moment in our olive-tree bowers, and often were we finally caught in the warm heavy splash.

The rain's first touch banishes for ever the golden transparency of burnt summer. Something is astir under the beautiful dry skeleton of last season's herbage ; and through it in a few days a down of fairest, lightest green is coming to life. At first it is only a gleam of silver alloy through the gold ; but no sunshine now can banish it, and soon it is all-conquering green.

Green buds open daily on grey and spiny thorns, and the few surviving flowers of summer's drought, monk's-hood, scabious, odd stars of myrtle, jasmine, oleander, etc., with abundance of thistles and some vari-coloured umbels, are soon buried in the joyous leap of many spring-like blossoms, till all thoughts of autumn are prorogued for a month at least, and the season verily appears as a topsy-turvy spring. There is such a bursting of fresh life everywhere; herbage and shrubs renewing their youth; peasants busy with greenest crops; little lambs following each family party to the fields; and a chorus of chattering and warbling birds arriving from Epiros.

The heavy summer heat is gradually replaced by a delicious air like our best English weather, and energy revives sufficiently to plan excursions.

By the second week in September the grey velvet broom stalks showed tiny leaf-buds, the incense plant hinted at its coming glory of gold, the various heaths showed colour, the first cyclamen appeared, and mauve autumn crocus outgrew the thin grass. A week later and the heaths were upstanding rose and crimson; and the darling *kopelluli* (little girls),—the most dainty and winning cyclamen, were tufting all the walls and stony ways, and making gay their chosen vineyards. Michaelmas daisies and purple sea lavender were on the marshes; gingellies were being gathered and dried, and fresh crops of sugar beet, sea kale, suchetti and melanzani were ripe. Driving to town one glimpsed a golden carpet of maize drying in some back-yard, or a group of variegated pumpkins making a pretty still-life group on a warm tiled roof. Vast quantities of tomatoes—at about 3½ lb. for 1d. (10 lepta) made fine scarlet patches on the roofs too. They are split and laid out to dry and then made into a conserve with salt for the winter.

The daisies are of quite unbelievable glory at this season, in woods and wastes their myriads stand a foot from earth and take the light as airily as cow parsley.

First the mauve, then the white autumn crocus comes out, veritably under foot, even on the main road ; for there is no end to Corfu's audacity of flowering. By the end of the month we can go down into one favoured wood where the wild narcissus grows : truly a poet's flower, if ever was one. It is the most fairylike of all Corfu's miniatures, and, with its scent, must surely come from some finer earth than ours.

In October the Japanese medlar (loquat) opens its pretty blossoms to scent the air, and there are wild roses and lady's tresses, orchis and dahlias, morning glory and chrysanthemums and jonquils and many another fair blossom ; and the days become absurdly short for such summer array and warmth.

In November we go down to another wood where real snowdrops spring among the olive roots. No different from our northern flower, though rather slenderer.

Many of these flowers, with beautiful roses, carnations and others, last through the tearing autumn gales and live to greet the first irises, anemones and jonquils of spring. So that on Christmas Day we garnered a posy of many seasons. There was a cyclamen from September and a last surviving snowdrop. There were

The Approach of the Vintage

February's blue irises and three kinds of jonquil, cinqfoil, mustard, a scrap of bugloss, corn marigold, orange and lemon blossom, yellow vetch, large pink clover (of April and May), ground ivy, scabious and *wild roses*, but no violets !

We have now outrun autumn. Let us go back to its chief event—the vintage.

Those early rains enriched the vineyards to a heavy crop, very beautiful to see. We half lived on grapes before the vintage. Afternoon tea was a leisurely stroll through one vineyard or another to take one's choice of the delicious fruit—and the variety is astonishing even in these small estates. The deep blue thick-skinned wine-grapes we ignored, for they would keep a month or two after the vintage. But there were rich purple grapes and delicate mauve ; sweet little golden amber and ice-green varieties with tight-packed translucent berries ; huge crimson *rothiti*, a wonderful colour with the sun through them ; and most delicate of all, the rose-crimson *robola*, a glowing wonder of bloom and transparency. These were all scattered about the vineyards, with no doubt many other shades and variations known only to a native. About the houses and courts were muscatels and lisabetta and suchlike specialities for the table. But even the commonest are delicious, so ripe and fresh. Heaped dishes of the varicoloured fruit adorned each meal, and their tints added to the gorgeous colouring of the market stalls.

127

An Artist in Corfu

Vintage begins about the third week in September, and its special stir and excitement are felt in town and country. For the most town-loving of Corfiotes must then, if at no other season, visit his estates to see to the wine-making. Town is emptied—country becomes animated. The peasants seem to undertake the vintage work with quite an appropriate spirit of enjoyment; the proprietors, perhaps not so joyfully. Many of the much-divided estates are so poor as barely to repay attention, consequently they receive none. Their little villas are so primitive and neglected that to our western ideas they would not be possible even for a three weeks' camp; and the owners themselves, when in the country, relapse into ways and clothes of quite startling antiquity.

The preparations for the gathering take about a week, and the special feeling of vintage begins when the great locked doors of the magazine begin to stand open, and the huge vats and butts are dragged out for repairs and scouring. As the oldest wood makes the best wine, these receptacles are caulked and patched and bound up to the last extremity, and then water and gravel are put in them, and for a day or two they are rolled on timbers by a couple of men in the courtyard.

The magazine—general store, lumber and box-room of the establishment—is meanwhile cleared and set in order, vanishable goods removed to other locked doors, and when all is prepared the gathering begins.

The Gathering of the Grapes

It is most exciting, but lasts far too short a time. It took eight women three days to harvest the Dousmani's grapes, and they worked quickly.

It is still very hot in September, and a vineyard is hotter than any other piece of earth ; and I seemed to spend the whole of those three days racing after the quickly moving, often vanishing group.

The gathering is a very pretty sight. The women are still in their light summer garments, and over their white wimples wear quantities of cloths or blanket to keep off the sun. They work in a line across a vineyard, under the eye of an overseer, cutting the grape stalks with the strong curved knives which they carry stuck in the back of their girdles, and finding time, in spite of speed and heat, for a lot of chattering and some munching.

Under the drying leaves the blue wine grapes hang like velvet. The vineyards have lost their summer greens and are almost russet in the clear sunlight. The little groups of women fairly twinkle with colour as they swiftly strip the vines, then raising the wide bloom-laden baskets to their heads, go with easy movement up the steps and terraced hillsides to empty their burdens into the high vats in the magazine; or, if distant, into a dusky heap in olive shade, awaiting a donkey's panniers.

The second vat is nearly full by the end of the first day's gathering. The first is heaped full, and from sheer weight of fruit the must begins to force its way through the primitive bamboo spigot.

An Artist in Corfu

Next morning a strong, lithe young man begins the treading. A shirt is his sole garment, and that is knotted to his thighs, and his long limbs are soon deep crimson. He begins by carefully treading a small hole to stand in, and then works into it the grapes piled above the rim. The spigot is of course uncorked now, and the must comes out in a strong opaque crimson spurt. It is drawn off into another large vat by means of a tin "jar" measure standing in a long wooden trough. The beautiful colour of must stains the trough, and lacquers the tin, and seems to pervade all the dusky half-light of the magazine. The treader labours down and down in the great vat, till his scarlet face vanishes in the depths and only two crimson and grape-spattered hands are visible on the rim. He lifts and turns the pulpy mass with a board, till the sound is like the homely slosh of a wash-tub.

It is very hard work: two vats a day, five or six hours' treading of each vat. Now and again the man emerges, moist and panting, balances his turning-board on the lofty rim of the vat and perches there for a cigarette and a chat with some passing acquaintance, or peasant bringing his toll of grapes.

The treader is paid on piece-work. He gets 6 lepta per jar of must—about half a drachma an hour, or six or seven drachmæ per day, and his food. Very high wages, of course, for the work is skilled as well as exceedingly laborious. Some treaders become almost intoxicated with the fumes of must.

Treading the Wine

As each vat is finished, Cipi, the overseer, measures the must back into it again with the jar, and as it is for red wine, the skins, stalks, etc., are all left in. A heavy wooden lid, weighted with stones, is floated on top, and in a few hours all the leavings have risen under it into a solid crust through which the liquid is audibly and visibly fermenting. For a week or ten days the fermentation goes briskly on, sending its acid aroma through the house and out at the windows. The fermented must is then drawn off into the butts, which must be absolutely full, and there it remains still fermenting, for a month, the bung holes left open meanwhile and the butts carefully replenished every few days. The skins, etc, are wrung through a press to extract the remaining must,—which is, of course, of second quality,—and are then cast out in a heap, to be afterwards burned and returned to the land.

The ravished vineyards are a desolate sight, and it was sad to know that the season of quite unlimited grapes had now passed. We had carefully " bagged " many bunches of the choicer grapes for future use. We bagged the whole pergola of lady's finger grapes in the court, but the season was so wet that they did not keep as they ought to have done. The bags keep off wasps and their kin, and are made of half a newspaper and three pins and tied on with string—we found the *Scotsman* was the toughest.

There are several by-products of vintage, all very delectable. The simplest is mustelevria, a very delicious sweet or jelly made by boiling fresh must to half its bulk with semolina and a little spice. The paste is then poured out on plates, stuck with a few almonds, and either eaten fresh or cut up and dried for keeping.

Another little industry is the making of fig cake or sakofitus. This is a strictly home industry—the peasants are imported and made to wash first, and one does not buy sakofiti in the market. The late autumn figs are gathered when ripe, torn open and laid on some convenient wall-top to dry in the sun. After a few days they are taken indoors to await the vintage. They are then minced finely and kneaded in a trough with new must and coriander and black pepper and a bottle of mastike spirit and mixed spices " to taste." The result is formed into buns and spread to dry in the sun for some days. It is then well wrapped in walnut leaves and stored away for the winter. It is not considered ripe and mellow for a month or two, and when well made and judiciously flavoured is very good.

Ladies are busy making their famous preserves and syrups and crystallisations in this richest season of fruit. Cooks do not consider sweets and desserts are in their department—the mistress and the confectioner must provide them, and many ladies are experts and renowned for some specialty. One may excel at orange-flower preserve, another at morella syrup ; from Cephalennia comes a very elaborate and highly spiced quince cheese, extremely black and sticky, but very insinuating; or a delicious conserve of mastike and sugar arrives from somewhere else.

In a few days the household has recovered its wonted calm. The peasants always lose their heads at any small deviation from routine, and of course the excitement of vintage has been tremendous—so many strange people about, and extra meals to be provided at ir-regular hours. For all workmen, even plasterers and suchlike casuals about a house, must be fed.

So we settle down again, and the magazine is locked, and begins to accumulate its winter stores. Strings of tomatoes are hung to ripen, and about a hundred bunches of grapes are slung on bamboo rods across the magazine roof. Heaps of potatoes, onions, sweet potatoes, quinces and nuts appear, as uncertain weather drives peasants to harvest their crops. October is called " finish-of-fruit " season, and certainly, after the earlier abundance on the market-stalls, there is a sort of dullness, though grapes, melons, apples, quinces and pomegranates remain in profusion for some weeks to come. The whole range of autumn vegetables gradually takes the place of the gaudier fruits of Sep-tember. In that month the stalls showed a wonderful medley, great baskets of ruddy peaches and apricots, green honey-sweet figs, grapes of every degree, apples, pears, lemons, sacks of walnuts, almonds, chestnuts, donkey-loads of reddest tomatoes, all acting as chorus to the main theme of yellow melons. Cartloads of melons stacked in sun and shade on the stalls, barricades of them filling the little piazza in the town. Monster long yellow fellows they are. It took three of us five days to eat one. Water-melons also, with their pleasant harmony of pink and green slices.

I had some fun painting market stalls in town, about vintage time. It was very hot still and I went off in Babazo's absurd little trap, directly after the early bathe.—Babazo lives in the village and his trap is very cheap indeed, and so we endured its deficiencies; and Babazo himself shops for us very efficiently, so is doubly useful, and his bow is a marvel of elegance. But to travel by him is far from luxury, for the springs are lop-sided and sometimes *nearly* make one seasick; there is no back nor side to the seat, and a painful lack of cushion, so that the drive into town is just about the limit of endurance.

I first established myself at the big café by the sea-gate, just hoping I might have space to work. But lo!—the kindest consideration from all around—a chair and table at my disposal almost before I had arrived, and not a soul allowed to hang over or disturb me. The waiter took me in special charge. Sauntering soldiers used their canes on anything small enough, and language, I should judge, on larger intruders who pressed too closely.

At the fruit stalls, where I painted later, the owners were almost jealous. The offered seat was primitive enough, but their best, and a board was found to keep my shoes off the mud, most considerately; while a

THE MARKET-PLACE DURING THE TOMATO SEASON.

The Val di Ropa

voluble tongue and most bold splashings of water kept the curious from my chosen stall.

In one little street a confectioner, under whose arcade I sat, barricaded the whole of his pavement for two afternoons to give me light and air. And very glad was I to have that much breathing space in the heat, and with weird and awful undercurrents of odour. No one seemed to mind the barricade, or think it irregular. At another place a chemist put his lad on duty half an afternoon thinning off the swarms of school-children who squabbled for places about me. Really I have never had such universal kindness and considera-tion in street sketching. The man in the street is my very good friend.

We had one long day excursion into the Val di Ropa at full vintage time. It was a glorious day, the atmo-sphere perfect. The valley was quite pink in its distant levels, framed by bluest hills. There the vintage is mostly of peasant proprietors ; the groups are of only a few figures together ; too scattered to be much of a spectacle ; and the trains of horses and donkeys taking the grapes to the homesteads were regrettably dull, the panniers all carefully covered with cloth, and the men in ordinary European clothes.

But the landscape was a dream ; where the valley escaped cultivation the kruso (incense-plant) stood in the thick of its golden flowering ; in spite of the heat the air was fresh, and the atmosphere—imported direct from fairyland, I suppose. It was a dreadfully long voyage though, and the roads very choppy. The Babazo car rolled horribly.

In the intervals of vintage work the peasants are all very busy with their new crops. The usual vegetables —sugar beet, leeks, onions, turnips, potatoes, marrows, etc., etc. Along the road trot mountains of green tops from sweet potatoes, entirely covering the little donkeys, and trailing to the ground; and maize is being garnered and ground, leaving a most desolate stubble.

Presently the empty woods of summer are repeopled with peasant groups; their sheep and goats returned from the summer flocking, and fat and happy in the rich new pasturage. The peasants themselves are busy scratching up little *bunds* of dry leaves and loose earth, around the limits of each olive-tree, preparing, before the heavy rains arrive, for the falling of the fruit.

These tiny earthwork trimmings appear all over the woods like the handiwork of brownies. One finds queer little perversions and rearrangements of familiar pathways, and notices roadside gutters iniquitously ridged and stopped too, under some overhanging tree, that the dropping olives may not be storm-swept into alien property.

Peasants build anew their dry-stone walls, and others walk over them. In October the fig-leaves and vine twigs are garnered as fodder for the accommodating donkeys. The women tending their animals in the woods twirl as they go a spindle of wool or flax. They climb high, with strong bare feet, to slender branches for the fruit crops, and stoop as freely, unhampered by the beautiful full skirts, to the many little wild green things of the vineyards, which they value as vegetables.

In October the gingelly-trees are stripped of their pretty strings of yellow, red, and mahogany-varnished fruit, and their dainty green foliage is soon as golden as a birch-tree's. The remaining fig-leaves sit like pale butterflies of gold among the labyrinthine elephant-grey branches. The waste places are rich with massive heaths of rose and crimson, and with the pendulous globes and clusters of the strawberry shrub. Only the spent vineyards fail from Corfu's usual superlative beauty. The land is not tesselated with their golden patches, as one rather demands it should be. They die shabbily, in dull russets and rust.

We regretfully abandoned our olive-tree bowers at the beginning of October; for such heavy rain had fallen that their foot or two of twig mattress would never dry again. In November we put away thinnest summer clothing and welcomed a tiny wood-fire in the evenings, though more for cheering than for warmth. By then had vanished for the winter one of the lesser joys of Corfu,—the warm dry earth on which one could anywhere drop and sketch; and one had to be resigned to fierce wet gales, or periods of blankety cloud and purple gloom, between the sunny and most welcome intervals of fine weather.

Indeed the sun counts for very much in southern

climes, and in Corfu especially wintry weather is un-provided with comforts. Corfu is a queer little back-water altogether, and presents little bits of life, little corners of faith and superstition which one had too easily believed obsolete.

Not only are the peasants mediævally minded, but even general society seems to belong to former genera-tions. Our friend is surely very early Victorian who is so genuinely terrorised by our most foolish and amiable dog, and who has never slept with her window open (*we* could not sleep indoors at all in summer) for fear that some " bestia " presumably a moth, since there are no deadly winged beasts there, might enter.

Then of what age or century is the Corfiote fear of a fire ? Here are living people who will not pay a call in any house where may be a fire, for they would afterwards certainly catch cold on coming away from it. So, many Corfiote houses have no chimney at all but the big hood over the kitchen fornella, and to our ideas nothing could be more miserable than the damp and stuffy cold of their rooms. Winter air is of such chill and penetrating quality that old and invalid people must be Spartan or perish. We pay calls in thickest coats, congealing slowly from the feet up, and find our hosts dressed as for out of doors—sometimes even to their gloves ! Pitifully passive resisters—too little demanding of life of any kind.

CHAPTER VIII

Winter : Mostly about Town

WINTER is not altogether a miserable season in Corfu, though its devoted inhabitants refuse to alleviate it by any comforts, and indeed rather deny that Corfu has anything so disagreeable. In truth, it does not last long—witness the flowers—and between its raging days of rain and biting days of wind are always periods of glorious sunshine ; the air a miracle of clearness, and tonic with the opposite mountains' snow.

Then one can tramp untired for miles, and visit all the fascinating little hill villages that seemed so much too far in warmer weather. Out of the keen wind and in the sunshine, one can paint all day and be sunburnt at it.

When a donkey and boy were procurable I went off in state and luxury and many coats ; for the donkey is a pleasant way of going, not too quick, and picking its own way so entirely that one is free to watch everything instead of only one's feet. Nothing will prevent it trotting on the way home though, and for an amateur a pack-saddle is rather an unhappy eminence then. And I will not climb loose stone walls on donkey back ; I was not brought up to it.

As it was a good olive year donkey-boys soon became

haughty and exorbitant, and without a peasant the donkey of course was unmanageable—a creature of hearty determinations, that had never known bridle. So off I went on foot; my pack on my back, and an obliging young dog for escort. Delightful goings on crisp dewy mornings, and more delightful returns, late, cold, hurrying, with the panorama of the Straits and their mountains rose-red with sunset before me.

Except for the few show places and stereotyped drives, where of course the inhabitants are no better than in other tourist resorts, one can go alone anywhere. In those little out-bye villages I met with nothing but kindness and courtesy, and in later wanderings among suburbs and nearer villages of the town I was just as politely welcomed.

In one of those distant villages, I had in mind an outside staircase for viewpoint. But when I went there for sketching the whole establishment was away in the fields, except a dog tied in the court, and furiously resenting strangers. His chain was so short that I passed him safely, and established my self and dog on the little " landing " upstairs. I found the view as I had anticipated, and had been an hour at work before an old couple appeared. The position might have been awkward—a stranger in possession, a stranger's dog positively forbidding them their own stairs ! Of course my few words of Greek were quite inadequate for either apologies or explanations. However, the old people were perfectly sweet and charming. They seemed quite to enjoy my invasion, and were hospitable to their poor limits. They brought me out their best pillows and a form to sit on. They insisted on giving me oranges each day ; and oh, pathetic ! in return for a little parting gift, they would have pressed on me a portion of their small store of potatoes : no doubt a gift of much greater value than fruit in their eyes. Canella, the lean brown dog, loved us dearly too, poor starveling, for Kouski and I brought him each day a special chunk of bread, and we became quite friendly. That was a most peaceful pitch, for not a single boy dared brave Canella, though several were impelled to try. Their swarms hung about the gate, and yelled from the broken walls, but within was peace. Of course boys will be annoying in any land, but so long as a grown-up was at hand I was never bothered by them in Corfu.

Another old acquaintance I made was at Potamo, three miles out of town. A village set among famous orange groves, and a very beautiful spot indeed. I was straying about as usual in by-ways, and went deep among the cool green orchards, lamp-lit with their golden fruit. The ancient owner found me, but, like the couple at Kalafationes, took my intrusion most affably, with neither surprise nor resentment. He sped me each day with clusters of oranges, and cordially invited me to go on a festa day, when he would have time to take me to a favourite viewpoint of his on the hill behind. I am still sorry that that day never came.

An Artist in Corfu

I spent some weeks of the new year sketching in and about town, never quite mastering the intricate warren inside the walls. Like all old walled towns, Corfu was packed and squeezed to its utmost capacity before modern security allowed expansion outside. The houses stand four or five stories high, with merest twisted passage-ways between. One day a friend and I each spent half an hour looking for the Venetian well;* without finding either it or each other, though we both knew where it ought to be, and had been there before.

The mark of Venice's four hundred years is strong on the town. All the old part is flavorous of Italy; its arcaded streets and cavernous cook-shops, its decayed mansions over squalid courts, even the popular cookery, is as much of Italy as of Greece, and the Greek vernacular is thick with Italian fragments. All the old town is picturesque, and I think only the Hebraica is too poisonous for an artist; for it is well kept, for a southern place. It is a pity the Jew quarter is so bad, because there one sees the men embroidering all the brilliant festa clothes of peasant women, and the colour in the dark open-fronted shops is very rich and interesting.

The old Ghetto was demolished in 1535, but the Hebraica is still distinctly the Jewish quarter, and the old prejudice against the Hebrews still lingers. They are cleverer workmen and more industrious than the Corfiotes, so it is likely to continue.

* La Cremosti, a handsome relic of the 17th century.

FORTEZZA VECCHIA.

The Venetian Forts

Numerous campanile rise from the town, but none are specially distinguished ; and the interiors of the churches likewise are often disappointing ; box-like, empty spaces, of plastered walls and no architectural features. Sometimes the screen is well wrought and in pleasing proportions, and the conventional figures of its panels—each in the special place designed for it in the rubrics—make a good pattern of gold and dark varnished colours. Of course such famous shrines as S. Spiridione, S. Teodora (the cathedral), and Paleokastrizza have beautiful ancient church plate, and their hanging lamps of silver are magnificent. Such churches have usually some ancient pictures on their walls ; the frames at any rate handsome enough to be worth seeing, and the paintings interesting archaically.

The really notable features of Corfu are the fine old Venetian forts. The square block of the Fortezza Nuova (c. 1580) stands just over the fishing port, a capable and efficient looking defence. But it is the great double-headed rock of the Fortezza Vecchia,— jutting its bold crests far beyond the town into the Straits—that is the unforgettable feature of the place, and that has fitly given its name * to the island. No doubt this rocky promontory has been fortified from earliest times. Its position—both locally to the island and racially to the factions of east and west—insists on that. But the existing fortifications are chiefly from Venetian times. Corfu was the principal arsenal

* The Byzantine name Κορυφώ. Κορυφαι, two peaks.

of Venice for her Levantine possessions, and it was due to her thorough strengthening of the natural defences of the town that Corfu, alone of all Greece, resisted every attack of the conquering Turks.

The town is separated from the outstanding peninsula of the Fortezza Vecchia by the width of the esplanade, nearly a quarter of a mile, and it was not walled till the rising tide of Turkish conquest threatened to engulf it at the beginning of the sixteenth century.

The Turks had made an unsuccessful attack on Corfu in 1431, and did not come again until the terrible siege of 1535, when they laid waste the island for thirteen days.

Here is Mr. Miller's graphic account of their invasion.*

". . . For a whole generation the Ionian islands enjoyed, like the other Venetian colonies, the long peace.

" At last, however, after rather more than a century of almost complete freedom from attack, Corfu was destined to undergo the first of the two great Turkish sieges, which were the principal events in her annals during the Venetian occupation. In 1537 war broke out between the republic and Suleyman the Magnificent, at that time engaged in an attack upon the Neapolitan dominions of Charles V. During the transport of troops and material of war across the channel of

* From " *The Latins in the Levant*," William Miller, page 559.

The Turkish Invasion

Otranto, the Turkish and Venetian fleets came into hostile collision, and though Venice was ready to make amends for the mistakes of her officials, the sultan resolved to punish them for the insults to his flag. He was at Valona, on the coast of Epiros, at the time ; and, removing his camp to Butrinto, whose commander surrendered at his approach, he gave orders for the invasion of Corfu.

" The island was not taken unawares. The presence of the Sultan in Epiros, and the naval operations of Andrew Doria to the north and south of Corfu, had put the authorities on their guard, and Admiral Girolamo Pesaro with a large fleet, which was joined by a contingent of five Ionian galleys, had been despatched to Corfiote waters. The town still relied for its protection on the two fortified peaks of what is now called the Fortezza Vecchia, defended by a garrison of some 2000 Italians and the same number of Corfiotes, and under the command of Naldo, an officer who had distinguished himself in the Italian wars, while four galleys, with their crews on board, lay behind the breakwater below the fortress. The place was well supplied with guns and ammunition ; it contained provisions for three years, and its defences were strengthened by the destruction of 3000 trees in the suburbs, which might have served as cover for the enemy.

" The Turks, under the command of the redoubtable Khaireddin Barbarossa, the most celebrated captain in the service of the Sultan, landed at Govino, where the much later Venetian arsenal now stands, towards the end of August, destroyed the village of Potamo, and marched upon the capital. On the 29th another force of 25,000 men crossed over to join him, these operations being facilitated by the fact that Pesaro had sailed up the Adriatic without engaging the Turkish fleet. The mart, as it was called, which lay outside the city walls, was speedily taken, and its remaining inhabitants found the gates shut against them and were forced to crouch under the castle ramparts on the rocky promontory of S. Sidero or behind the breakwater. The Corfiote traveller Noukios, an eye-witness of the siege, has left a graphic account of the sufferings of these poor wretches, huddled together on a narrow ledge of rock, without food or shelter, and exposed to the stones of the garrison, and to the full force of one of those terrific storms of rain not uncommon* in Corfu at that season. Those who could afford to bribe the soldiers on the walls were pulled up by means of ropes, while the rest were left to die of cold or hunger. When it seemed that the siege was likely to last, the Venetian governor, in order to economise food and space, turned out of the fortress the old men, women, and children, who went to the Turkish lines to beg for bread. The Turkish commander, hoping to work on the feelings of the garrison, refused ; so the miserable creatures, repudiated alike by the besieged and the besiegers, wandered about distractedly between the two armies,

---

* Corfiotes deny the frequency !

striving to regain admission to the fortress by showing their ancient wounds gained in the Venetian service; and, at last, when their efforts proved unavailing, lying down in the ditches to die. Meanwhile, for three days and nights the suburbs were blazing, and the Turks were ravaging the fair island with fire and sword. The castle of Sant' Angelo on the west coast alone resisted their attacks. More than 3000 refugees from the countryside had congregated within its walls, and four times did its brave Corfiote garrison repulse the enemy. Barbarossa, whose headquarters were at the Avráme Palace on the sea-shore, now began the bombardment of the fortified peninsula, which contained the mediæval city of Corfu. He planted a cannon on the islet of Vido, then called Malipiero, the plesaunce of a nobleman, and noted for its abundance of game. But the gunners made such bad practise that in three days they only hit the mark five times, while the rest of their shots flew over the fortress into the sea on the other side. Nor was Barbarossa more fortunate in an attempt to bombard the city from his own galley; a well-aimed shot struck the vessel, and, when he retired in the direction of the fountain of Kardaki, where ships were accustomed to water, and began a cannonade of the place from that side where the walls were lower, the great distance caused most of his projectiles to fall short of the mark. At this, Ayas Pasha, the grand vizier, resolved to see for himself the prospects of taking the city; he therefore ventured out one dark and rainy night to inspect the moat and the walls. What he saw convinced him that Corfu could only be captured after a long siege, whereas the month of September had now begun and sickness had broken out among the half-starved Turks. He therefore advised the Sultan to abandon the attempt. Suleyman first resolved to try the effect of persuasion upon the garrison ; he therefore sent a Corfiote prisoner to frighten the Venetian authorities into surrender. The bailie, Simeone Leone, and the provveditore, Luigi da Riva, dismissed the Sultan's envoy without a reply, and a brisk cannonade from the castle batteries proved an effective answer to fresh demonstrations of hostility. Suleyman therefore made a virtue of necessity ; the grand vizier sent for the Venetian representative at Constantinople, who was at the Sultan's headquarters, and offered to raise the siege, if the republic would compensate his master for his losses ; but before any reply could arrive from Venice, the siege had been already raised. After firing all the houses that remained standing in the suburbs, the Turks were ordered to embark ; their fleet made one more demonstration, but on the 11th September, after a stay of only thirteen days in the island, they recrossed the channel to Epiros. But in that short time they had wrought enormous damage. The Corfiote traveller tells us that they had destroyed " all the works of men's hands " throughout the island, and that they slew or carried off all the animals they could find ; sparing only the trees and vines, owing to the suddenness of their departure. The Duke of Naxos wrote to the Pope, that two large cities might have been built out of the houses and churches which they had destroyed ; the privileges and letters-patent of the islanders had perished in the flames or had been used as ammunition, and a Corfiote petition states that they carried away more than 20,000 captives. The population was so greatly reduced by this wholesale deportation, that the nobles had to be recruited from the burgesses, and nearly forty years afterwards the whole island contained only some 17,500 inhabitants, or less than one fifth of the estimated population in classical times. . . . "

There was another great Turkish siege in 1716, notable as the Turks' last great effort at conquest in Christendom ; when the brave and skilful soldier of fortune, Marschall Schulemberg, whose statue still adorns the esplanade, fought the whole military and naval power of the Ottoman empire for six weeks. The Turks arrived with sixty ships of war and numerous smaller vessels on July 5th, and the General-in-chief had 30,000 picked troops landed from the fleet at Govino (which was used by the Venetians as a light draught harbour). The Venetian fleet arrived on the 8th, but the Turks were forewarned of its approach by the sound of a salute to the famous Shrine of Our Lady of Kasoppa, across Govino Bay, and the two fleets stood at bay without any decisive sea-fighting. The Turks of course commanded the landing. The General established himself at Potamo and ravaged the country far and wide—the terrified peasantry fleeing into the town. The Turks soon possessed the suburbs, and there was much desperate fighting and great loss on both sides. It is said that even priests and women helped to defend the town walls. Before dawn on the 19th a grand assault left the Turks in possession of an outwork of the Fortezza Nuova, but Schulemberg in person headed a desperate sortie, and drove them back with immense loss. By the 22nd the Turks had retreated, abandoning stores, ammunition and artillery, and it is said losing half their army in action and by disease, while the Venetians lost 2000 of their garrison of 5000.

Some parts of Fortezza Veechia date from this period ; what is now called the Fortezza Nuova was built between 1577 and 1588, when the new defences were completed.

The forts were all dismantled at the English withdrawal from Corfu in 1864 ; there is grass on their causeways now ; the English barrack is a hospital much too large for its population ; and no guns but salutes of honour wake the echoes of the bay that has heard so many.

Little clusters of khaki conscripts come to drill and run about on the esplanade in the mornings, and there are occasional cricket matches when a British man-of-war puts in ; but the whole place is asleep : the peaceful chimney-corner sleep of the very old.

All the society of Corfu is within the town, hardly

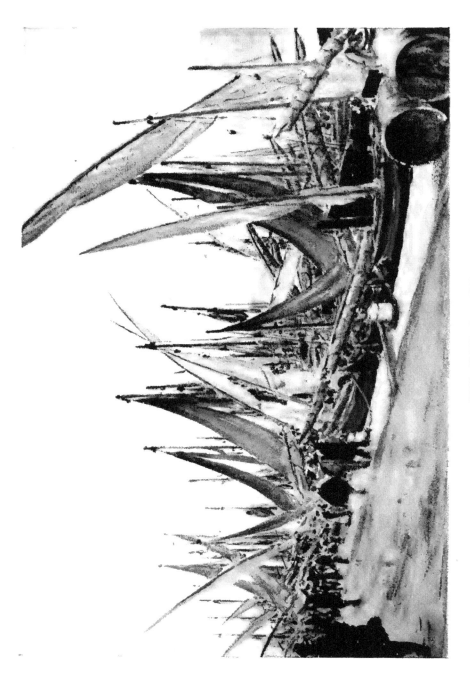

THE FISHING PORT.

Corfiote Society

spreading even to the suburbs, but all the society is very little, and one must not expect the finest quality of brain either to come or to stay within the limitations of a backwater.

In theory Corfiotes admire their island immensely, and in practice many of them cannot be happy away from it. But the most enthusiastic will not live outside the town ; only necessity or the very hottest weather will drive them to stay in the country. The few eccentrics who do live on their estates are conse-sequently much isolated, and the average Corfiote has rarely much real knowledge of the island. Often they have not travelled beyond the district of their own estates, and as for the wonderful riches of the flowers—well, flowers are mostly " wild," and therefore unregarded.

One day I asked a girl—educated in England, too—the name of the stately hot-weather lily (eremurus) which was growing thickly just outside her gates. She pondered awhile and then said, " It is a daffodil," and she was not wider of the mark than most of whom one asks information ! A lady who wishes to impress you as *very* advanced and so on, will tell you she likes wild flowers—just as she will feel superior because she sleeps with an open window. We are only a generation ahead. Still, it seems strange.

It is all very well to have theories about drains ; but southerners do manage to live where, by the theories of northern sanitarians, they should speedily die. True,

An Artist in Corfu

they do not look extremely well, but the climate has something to say to that, and they have diseases, but so have we, in spite of sanitary theories. And many of them live to a great age.

Two dear old friends of mine lived over a mews— entered from it, too. Yes, it was dreadful—but they lived. Another, this in the front street, too, said she could not open her windows in summer as the air was too bad, and she had moved to this house because her son had nearly died of typhoid in the last.

However, Corfu is sweet and well kept compared to many southern towns, and the hotels are quite modern and do not suffer from the defects of the old town.

In the winter some little Italian opera company comes for a season, with an ancient and limited repertoire, and every one has a box at the nice little theatre, chiefly for social purposes. It is an unending wonder to me how little the Corfiotes demand of life. Why not newer music ? why not a cool mountain hotel in stifling summer ? why not fireplaces in winter ? better drainage ? They have no capital in the island, and all the fertility of it seems useless against the want of initiative in the educated, and the primitiveness of the peasant. Indeed Corfu keeps its luxuriance in spite of its inhabitants, rather than because of them.

Though Venice was wise enough to encourage agriculture, she would not forego authority in her possessions, and to keep under the native nobility she forbade them all trade, made education a farce, and obliged them

The Corfiote Ladies

to live in town if they would claim the small share of government and power allowed them. So that in the end agriculture was not helped but ruined, for the gentry forgot how to live on their estates, and the land was and is left to the traditional and undeveloped methods of the peasant. The undeveloped mind is amazing, through a long period of acquaintance. There is such a hopeless wrongness and lack of reason in its workings, such a capacity for damage and blundering in any work not straitly ruled by custom, that one continues wondering how anything beautiful or useful is left on the island. For example, Lennè will tether the donkey within cord's length of a young and treasured pergola of vines, within two days of a severe scolding for having left him on the margin of a vineyard. Sheep will be left to browse on the struggling seedlings in the garden, or their cords to chafe a grove of baby cypresses, or the tender shoots of young fig-trees. Corfu must sometimes have hard work against its inhabitants !

The days of the Corfiote ladies are a little mystery which I have not penetrated. They live in flats, so there is not much housework. I have rarely seen a book in any room ; perhaps their very fine needlework and very excellent conserves occupy them. In the late afternoon or evening they dress with great care and elaboration :—Corsetted amazingly, gowned if possible from Paris, their splendid hair perfectly dressed, and with most impressive hats, they take the air on the esplanade, see their friends, and sit late in the cafés in the hot weather. Even in summer they do not relax the rigours of their toilette. They usually speak several languages well, but the whole island is strikingly devoid of books. A few ultra-energetic spirits visit and help the hospital and prison, but that is considered rather remarkable. Family affairs seem the sole interest of the women, as politics are of the men. One is drearily oppressed by such indifference and feels that the most extravagant flannelled-fooling is better and more hopeful. The place is too old perhaps and its very desires are dying.

There are six or seven members of Parliament for Corfu, and to minimise corruption they must each solicit the suffrage of the whole island, instead of standing for different districts. I believe they tour the island in a gang; at any rate, the less accessible parts. It seems a cumbersome and exhausting arrangement, and I have not heard that corruption is yet extinct. Manhood suffrage came very early to the uneducated peasants of new Greece, many of whom cannot read and write at the present day, and whose minds are still extraordinarily undeveloped. To these a vote is, naturally, regarded as something personally useful, even to be openly auctioned for personal gain, or at best, to be used for some entirely local advantage. That their M.P. should procure them a road, or contrive that sentence passed should not be executed on their cousin the murderer, is the nearest approach one can expect to patriotism. Local counsellors may be profitably elected on such terms. But they are disastrous for a nation : its leaders too dependent on satisfying the local needs of their constituents to achieve a national policy.

It seems to belong to the national temperament that the party system tends to become rather a strife of personalities than of principles. And as every little office-boy, yea, even a half-finished contract, is changed with change of ministry, small office holding with its degrading influences wastes the resources of the country. The intense patriotism and philanthropy of many over-seas Greeks, which are dowering Greece so richly with schools and public institutions, seem of small avail against the general and immemorial inability to amalgamate in a truly national spirit. Famous business men abroad, at home they cannot even run a postal system. Even between Athens and Corfu— the main route to commercial Europe—letters are constantly lost, or take any time from five days to a fortnight to do a journey of less than twenty-four hours.

This being the general condition it is not surprising to find woman is by law still very much a vassal.

If a woman leave her husband, even for his open and insulting unfaithfulness, she is still in his power. He may live as he likes, and go where he pleases, but she, a virtuous woman, may never appear in any public place of entertainment, may not attend a concert, nor leave her house for a single night—even to attend on illness or for any other serious reason—without the man's permission. *If she did*, he could divorce her ; and though she may long to be free, the divorce will make their children illegitimate if they have not attained their majority. Add to this, that no contract though written and sealed is binding between husband and wife, and the woman's subjection and insecurity is complete. The man might give her permission—to take a child abroad to school, for example—repudiate the agreement, and bastardise the child.

Needless to say it is only of very recent years that women have been bold enough to walk unattended in this mildest little town, where every one is a friend or relation. They accept Englishwomen's free ways, of course, but always with a wondering " are you not afraid ? "

CHAPTER IX

On Festas

ON the vigil of a great winter festa the little town of Corfu is as lively as an ant heap; peasants and townspeople alike busy providing for the coming holidays. The narrow streets are half blocked with stacks of fruit and vegetables, and overflowing stalls of all manner of provisions.

There are pyramids of endive, cauliflowers, and broccoli in all its charming and original shades of mauve, yellow and purple; enormous faggots of leeks and of all the good wild green things; masses of oranges and lemons glowing from their fresh shining leaves; stalls of dried fruits and nuts, and of cheeses dry and fresh; the sheep cheese, extracted from its unattractive preservative of slimy clay, still milk-white and excellent.

Sweet potatoes and chestnuts all hot; fried fish of many sizes and degrees, from lordly tunny to humblest miniatures; purple octopi and other things unclassable, are all a-cooking by the wayside.

The man wielding his spoon beside the huge cauldron of *fritelli* is an artist, and we pause to admire the masterly grace with which his forefinger flicks each morsel of curranty dough into its boiling bath, whence it emerges a golden and most popular mouthful.

Fascinating to youthful eye and tooth are the hawker's

baskets of ring-cakes, strung on rows of upright sticks in pink and white variety. A porridge of maize and winkles is also on the street menu, with other delicacies whose foundations are among the lesser mysteries.

Clean and attractive as the things appear, resident Corfiotes do not recommend them. Indeed I could a dreadful tale unfold, concerning a very celebrated brand of fritelli.

I think no shopkeeper north of Greece could find time to dispose his eggs so pleasingly among the partitioned fruits of his shop-cave and the stall emerging therefrom ; their scattered pattern of white retreats up to the dimmest corners. He also contrives a few flowers and bunches of fresh green leaves about the humblest cheese and fish stalls.

Amid the throng of people and crates there are peasants freeing themselves and their donkeys of their bulky loads of glossy greens, of brilliant fruits, or of little round turnips washed as white as the white Greek eggs. They spread out their passive fowls,—unfortunates which are always transported in living bunches by the legs ; they tether their equally unremonstrant turkeys, which may have run a long day's journey hither, or like the more miserable hens, have travelled, head dangling, on the outwork of a trap. I have even seen a double row of hens slung on the handle-bar of a bicycle. Busy cooks and housewives thread the crowd, followed by basket bearers. Fathers of families load themselves with armfuls of long bread, or with those lifebelt shaped loaves which are so much easier to carry with a general cargo; for the great festas of S. Spiridione, Christmas, and Epiphany are each of two days' duration, so shopping for them is quite a bulky business.

On the festa days proper hardly even a cavern in Fried-Fish Street is open, and any improvident stranger in the land must apparently live exclusively on coffee and mandolata. When one has seen the rapidly vanishing heaps of the latter delicious sweetmeat—a nougat of honey, almonds and white of egg—one can really believe that its manufacture at festa time accounts for a periodic scarcity of eggs in the island.

The indigenous sweets of Greece are very good, and have also the merit of genuineness, being often more in the nature of a sweet food than of our lollipops. There is one satisfying compound, halvas—of ground sesame seed and honey or sugar—which is regularly served to the soldiers as a daily ration during the long and strict lenten fast, and very alleviating it must be*.

No great entertainments mark the festas. The streets are as deserted as London on bank-holidays; empty but for the sound of church bells and drift of incense. The churches are all strewn with fresh leaves of daphne, and all day long people pass in to kiss the ikons and relics about the lamp-lit screens.

After Mass the town empties itself on the esplanade.

* The wedding cake of the ancients was made of sesame and honey. Strange that it should survive as a food for fasts.

An Artist in Corfu

How little the Corfiote asks of life ! He will stroll and chat through his holiday with no more thrilling entertainment than the band of the Philharmonica or a legal and open game of pitch and toss. And on work days he does not protest when all the Philharmonica (oh, misnamed !) practise their parts separately in one room in the main street, blasting the neighbourhood.

Though Christmas is a two days' feast, with as solemn a sacrifice of turkey as in England, it is New Year which is the special festival of children, when gifts are given and exchanged, and booths are full of the simple toys and gaudy edibles dear to youth.

In due course, and always reckoning by the old-style calendar, comes the Epiphany, the first great church festival of the New Year. There are still observed two separate and elaborate services for the blessing of the waters ; the first, on the night of the vigil, was originally for the baptism of catechumens, while the second, which, except in Corfu, takes place under the open sky, is on the morning of the festa proper, and is for the blessing of rivers, lakes, pools, and wells.

For this festa a bower of myrtle and other fresh green boughs is erected in the churches, and this enshrines a fount from which the consecrated water flows into basins to be received by the faithful. A very ancient crucifix is used in the service of sanctification at S. Spiridione, a much-kissed relic not six inches high.

During the days ensuing, the blessed water is borne

by the priests to each house in their parish, and each room is sprinkled, favourite plants even receiving a special portion.

The prayers used at these Epiphany services are very ancient and beautiful, being of St. John Chrysostom and St. Basil. They seem akin to the Psalms in their godly fear and richness of imagery. The service, as is usual in the Orthodox Church, is interspersed with short litanies.

The services of the Greek Church are extraordinarily varied, each great festa having special forms and observances, so that an orthodox service book is a weighty and complicated volume and is used chiefly by the priests, the congregation taking part only in the numerous litanies and prayers which are common to most of the services. The scriptures, epistles and gospels are read, as with us. But the Greek service book has a wealth of beautiful ancient prayers to which our church service has no parallel.

Here is the prayer of sanctification of the waters at the Epiphany (" The Jordan Festival ").*

" Great art thou, O Lord, and marvellous are thy works, and speech sufficeth not to sing the praise of thy wonders. (*Repeated three times.*)

"For thou, by thy will, from nothingness hast brought

* From the Service Book of the Holy Orthodox Church. Compiled, translated and arranged from the Old Slavonic Church Service Books of the Russian Churches and collated with the Service Books of the Greek Church by Isabel Florence Hapgood. (Houghton, Mefflins Co., The Russian Press, Cambridge, U.S.A., 1906.)

all things into being ; by thy majesty thou dost uphold all creation, and by thy providence thou dost direct the world. When thou hadst framed the universe out of four elements, thou didst crown the circle of the year with four seasons. All the reason-endowed powers tremble before thee. The sun singeth thy praises, and the moon glorifieth thee ; the stars also stand before thy presence. The light obeyeth thee. The deeps shudder with awe before thee ; the water springs do thy bidding. Thou hast spread out the heavens like a curtain. Thou hast established the earth upon the waters. With sand hast thou walled in the sea. Thou hast shed abroad the air for breathing. The Angelic Powers serve thee. The Archangelic Hosts adore thee. The many eyed Cherubim and the six-winged Seraphim, as they stand about and do fly, veil their faces with awe before thine unapproachable glory. For thou, the God which cannot be circumscribed, who art from everlasting and ineffable, didst come down upon earth taking on the form of a servant, and being made in the likeness of men.

" For thou couldst not endure, O Master, because of thy tender-hearted mercy, to behold the children of men tormented by the devil; but thou didst come, and didst save us. We confess thy grace ; we proclaim thy mercy ; we conceal not thy gracious deeds. Thou hast set at liberty the generations of our race, by thy birth thou hast sanctified a virgin's womb. All creation singeth praises unto thee, who dost reveal thyself ; for thou art our God, who hast been seen upon earth, and didst dwell among men. Thou didst hallow, also, the streams of Jordan in that thou didst send down from heaven thy Holy Spirit, and didst crush the heads of the serpents that lurked there. (*Then the priest repeateth, twice, the following, and blesseth the water with his hand at each repetition.*)

"Wherefore do thou, O King, who loveth mankind, come down now also through the inspiration of thy Holy Spirit, and sanctify this water. (*Thrice.*)

"And impart unto it the grace of redemption, the blessing of Jordan. (*Thrice.*) Make it a fountain of immortality, a gift of sanctification, a remission of sins, a healing of infirmities, a destruction of demons ; unapproachable by hostile powers, filled with angelic might. And may it be unto all those who shall draw it and shall partake of it, unto the purification of their souls and bodies, unto the healing of their passions, unto the sanctification of their houses, and unto every expedient service.

"For thou art our God, who through water and the Spirit dost renew our natures, which had fallen into decay through sin. For thou art our God, who with water didst drown sin in the days of Noah. For thou art our God, who by the sea, through Moses, didst set free from slavery to Pharaoh the Hebrew race. For thou art our God, who didst cleave the rock in the wilderness, so that water gushed forth, and who madest the floods to well forth abundantly ; and didst satisfy thy thirsty people. For thou art our God, who by fire and water, through Elijah, didst set Israel free from the errors of Baal.

" Do thou, the same master, sanctify now also this water by thy Holy Spirit. (*Thrice.*)

" Grant also unto all who shall be sprinkled therewith, and shall partake thereof, and shall anoint themselves therewith, sanctification, blessing, purification and bodily health.

" Save, O Lord, and show mercy upon the most holy Governing Synod, and keep them in peace beneath thy shelter. Subdue under them every foe and adversary ; grant unto them all their petitions which are unto salvation and life eternal ; that with the elements, and men, and Angels, and with all things visible and invisible, they may magnify thy most holy Name, together with the Father, and the Holy Spirit, now and ever, and unto ages of ages, Amen.

Priest. Peace be with you.

Choir. And with thy spirit.

Deacon. Bow your heads unto the Lord.

Choir. To thee, O Lord."

What a beautiful and reverent recognition of the power of God prepares the way for the petition of sanctification, and what a noble and confident uplifting of mankind is in the final aspiration.

I hesitate to give any longer quotations, but there are some sentences in a prayer of St. Basil for the

Some Beautiful Prayers

Sixth Hour, which I always think Stevenson must have known, and which seem to me extraordinarily vivid and beautiful :

"... Who by his precious cross didst destroy the handwriting of our sins. . . . Deliver us from every harmful and gloomy transgression. . . . Nail our flesh to the fear of thee, and incline not our hearts to words or thoughts of guile, but wound our souls with the love of thee. . . ."

Surely " the Celestial Surgeon " had ancestry here.

Another gem from the rich store is a little prayer of St. Ephraim the Syrian :

" O Lord and Master of my life, grant not unto me a spirit of slothfulness, of discouragement, of lust of power, of vain babbling.

" But vouchsafe unto thy servant the spirit of continence, of meekness, of patience, and of love.

" Yea, O Lord and King, grant that I may perceive my own transgressions, and judge not my brother. For blest art thou unto ages of ages. Amen. "

The symbolism and rubrics of the Church are too elaborate to be touched on except by a specialist ; even the rubric of bell-pealing is detailed and complicated ; and the shape of all the church, its furnishings and utensils are all full of meaning, though I imagine much is forgotten by the congregation. The tripledoored screen bars the Holy of Holies from unordained men, and from all women ; while in former days women were allowed only in the screened galleries at the west

165

end of the church.

The orders of angels are still believed in and invoked ; the angels keep their ancient places as " the honourable bodiless powers of Heaven." Here is a short hymn :—

"O ye chieftains of God, Servitors of the Divine glory, Guides of Men and Captains of the Bodiless Powers : Entreat that which is profitable for us, and great mercy ; in that ye are the Chieftains of the Bodiless Powers."

The Virgin is invoked as " Queen over all and Maiden of God. . . . Mother of the everlasting light, Hail Queen, thou glory of Motherhood, Maidenhead . . . Mother of Life . . . Abode of thy Maker illimitable."

The Litanies are so very varied and beautiful that it is impossible to select from them. One short extract must end this digression. It is one of the four Exorcisms of the Devil at baptism :—

"Preserve the child . . . from every poison and perplexity, from every storm of adversity, and from evil spirits, whether of the day or of the night . . . and hedge her round about with bright and shining angels, and preserve her from every invasion of evil spirits . . . and from the evil eye."

A very deliberate care for detail here guards the infant from every variety of evil and seems a characteristic of the church.

The Greek services must surely have been made for more diligent or more patient worshippers than are we of the west ; for with long prayers and chantings

The Feast of Feasts

and responses, with repetitions and exorcisms and litanies, they often run on for a couple of hours or more. The while, the congregation must stand, for only the more important churches have even a few stalls or miserere stools against their walls, and there is never a pew or bench for the weary.

To the blessing of village wells at this season, the villagers go in procession with their priests. Corfiotes are very particular in this respect, for the island's droughts are serious and damaging and frequent enough to be had ever in remembrance. But perhaps the abundant fishing of their coasts is cause for Corfiotes, alone of all Greeks, omitting the blessing of the sea.

Easter is called " the feast of feasts " in the Greek Church; no other approaches it in importance; and it is preceded by the longest fast of all the abstemious Greek year. Forty-six days all told, for the *forty days' fast* finishes before Palm Sunday, and then there is the *fast of Holy Week*. It is a complicated fast, for the *forty days* is again preceded by *meat-fast week*, during which the animal products of cheese, milk, butter and eggs are permitted, but no flesh.

No animal products are allowed during the first and last weeks of the great fast, nor on each Wednesday and Friday of it; and some people keep this strict rule for the whole forty-six days. On Good Friday even oil is prohibited, and the rule on this day seems quite universally kept. Though within the last two years the Greek rule has been modified almost to the leniency of the Roman, the peasants continue in the ancient unindulged regime.

In some ill-prospered parts the poor folk have been known to ask their priests to make more fasts—"*for it is easier to go hungry then*"!

Though many of the educated have outgrown the salutary rule of the fast, few Corfiotes have abandoned the sacrifice of the Passover lamb at their threshold; wherefore the reddened doorposts and ghoulish sights of the streets are to be avoided on Easter Eve.

Lamb and dancing are the unchanging and only entertainments of the peasant. Weather permitting, the villages dance even at the winter festas, but it is at Easter that the season of village balls really begins, when costumes of flaming brilliance collect under wayside olives and circle kaleidoscopically in the main streets.

On Easter the villages dance for two days, with a staying power known only to peasants; and amazing quantities of lamb are disposed of by people who know the hunger of the lean years when olives fail. No village festa is complete without an adequate supply of the long spitted bodies, each slowly turned by a small boy, over embers on the earth. When the thing is cooked its proprietor stands in those alpine attitudes to which the long spit lends itself, and just cuts the body shorter and shorter till all is consumed.

The peasant who makes his daily meal of bread

STA. BARBARA. POTAMO.

Bridal Dances

alone, with a trifle of oil or cheese, maybe, or of garlic and greens, but oftenest just bread, will take his feast of too solid flesh, equally without accompaniment. And of lamb that has had a name, too, and a red braid for its neck. Alack the day when fate's rough hand seizes any portion of its young anatomy that comes to hand, and hurries it to the slaughter.

As spring festas are fashionable seasons for peasant weddings, bridal dances are numerous from Easter onwards; so in the larger villages, if it is not a poor year, there will be a dance of some kind nearly every Sunday. The bride on these occasions is expected to dance through the programme, a feat of endurance through which she is probably sustained by the eclipsing splendour of her costume. For, added to the normally elaborate and distinguished coiffure, the bride wears a massive wreath of gay ribbons, tinsel, and small varicoloured flowers; and her muslin bollia, instead of dropping in soft folds, is stiffened high above all this, and scattered with drops of gold and flowers. The fine stitchery of her full white smock is hidden under a shower of light gold ornaments, and her velvet and gold embroidered vest and jacket are the richest and newest.

As bridehood continues from the time of betrothal till after the marriage, there may be quite a bevy of these resplendent damsels clustered in the van of the women's chain; those of lesser glory are towards the rear, and a fringe of little uncoiffed girls and children clings at the skirts.

Besides the great festivals universal to Christ, the Virgin, and the great saints, different districts and villages have festas commemorating their own special patrons. These local *panegyrie* are rather different from the rest, more in the nature of rustic fairs to which the neighbourhood gathers. Gastouri has its *panegyrie* for the nativity of the Virgin (September 8th o.s.), patroness of the chief church of the village. There are about eight other chapels, all served by the two village priests. There are booths of painted gingerbread, and ring cakes galore, and sweets and wine, and of course many roast lambs. And a bit of a band from town, unfortunately, because we are very up-to-date in Gastouri. But Gastouri cannot dance to the opera tunes, and the town musicians drown their country cousins' airs of mandoline and guitar, so the band is a regrettable and cacophonous innovation.

There is a great *panegyrie* at the feast of the Ascension, held on a high green sward overlooking the sea between Mon Repos and the Canone. As the most ancient ruins in the island are about this spot, and it could not be more beautifully adapted to its purpose, imagination may be allowed a long stretch backwards for the origins of this assembly. But it is so near town that much of its distinctive character is now lost in the nondescript crowd of spectators.

The most beautiful *panegyrie* I have seen is that

A Panegyrie

held in a grove of wonderful ancient olives at Mesonghi
beyond Benizza, on the festa of St. Constandinos,
May 3rd. We came to it in the afternoon, passing
groups of lustily singing and steadily tramping peasants
from the more distant villages, barefoot and carrying
their shoes, a blaze of colour on the blazing road.

We found the centre of the wood alive with circles
of dancers ; its outskirts sprinkled with their donkeys
and horses ; groups of peasants resting about the
giant boles of the olives, and numerous little boys
acting turnspit to whole and horrible lambs.

The Lefkimme women who come from the south
wear bollias of orange and yellow instead of the white
muslin of our district, gold embroidery all but hides
the coloured velvet of their coats and vests, and their
skirts are of shot silk of green and purple and blue,
with the gayest and most coquettish muslin aprons.
Some have six silver balls, as big as fair-sized apples,
hung from the right front of their jackets, in over-
grown but pleasing symbolism of buttons.

The secret magic of the olive-trees was in the light ;
and through the blue drift of wood smoke and the
enchanted sunlight the picture leapt from the ethereal
glamour of a Watteau into the daring colours of modern
Spanish painters, and again receded into the dim en-
chantment of a fairy tale. Who knows in what
dynasty of fairies was such a festa begun !

171

CHAPTER X
Saint Spiridione

MORE important to the Corfiotes than any other feste are the great feast-days of S. Spiridione, patron of all Corfu, and a saint most potent and revered throughout and beyond the island.

Saint Spiridione was a shepherd, who after the death of his wife became a monk, and finally Bishop of Trimython, his birthplace in Cyprus. He was one of the fathers at the famous council of Nicæa, A.D. 325, and it is recorded that there he gave miraculous testimony to the disputed doctrine of the Holy Trinity; for a brick which he held in his right hand was suddenly hurled to the ground and from it a stream of water and fire burst forth, thus demonstrating the Trinity in unity.

Other miracles are recorded of him later, so that when he died in 350, at over ninety years of age, it is natural that his relics were greatly treasured. He was buried in Cyprus, but after a hundred and one years his body was exhumed because of the sweet-smelling evaporation that came from the tomb, and was kept for two hundred years in his church at Trimython.

When Cyprus fell to the Saracens, the holy corpse was transported to Constantinople, and when that city also fell to the Moslems in the Turkish conquest of 1453, " George Kalaichairetis, a priest, and a wealthy and honoured citizen of Constantinople, took thought how to preserve the bodies of St. Spiridion and of St. Theodora Augusta, which were then both reposing in his church. He put the bodies into two sacks of straw, placed these on a mule, and led them safely through the devastated Greek country, easily persuading any people he met on the way, that his mule's burden contained nothing but the animal's food."

George remained with his sacred charge at Paramythion on the opposite coast of Epiros till 1456, when he brought the two bodies to Corfu and placed them in the church of the Archangel Michael.

During the siege and subsequent alterations in the town the relics were always carefully guarded from harm and risks, and finally in 1595 S. Spiridione was installed in the newly completed church bearing his name, where he has been worshipped with due honours ever since ; while S. Theodore was placed in the Cathedral, where she also is still enshrined.

When the priest, George Kalaichairetis died, his property—the embalmed saints, for we hear nothing of other riches—was divided among his three sons, the two elder sharing St. Spiridione, while the youngest took St. Theodora. The last, however, subsequently gave his relic to the community in 1483.

George's eldest son, Philip, a priest, inherited his younger brother's share of S. Spiridione in 1489, and was then commissioned to take the body to Venice; but the tears and entreaties of the Corfiotes prevailed and the project was abandoned.

When Philip died, a half share of S. Spiridione fell to his widow and his little daughter Asimène, and the other half to his brother Luke (the youngest, who had possessed and given away S. Theodora). The latter subsequently gave his share as a wedding gift to the said Asimène, who thus became sole heritress of this so carefully bequeathed saint.

Asimène, with no other dowry than the saint, was in 1527 wooed and wed by Stamation Boulgaris, a noble Corfiote, and by her will left the sacred relic to the children of this marriage and to their descendants in perpetuity, so long as one in the family should be a priest.

Thus it happens that S. Theodora belongs to Corfu, but S. Spiridione belongs to the Boulgaris to this day. And, in taking the dowerless Asimène Kalaichairetis, Stamation gave to his heirs the most precious possession in Corfu, and the church of the richest offerings.

For, shortly after his arrival in the island, S. Spiridione began to manifest his special patronage of the Corfiotes by miraculous cures of his suppliants, and the shrine became a famous place of pilgrimage, and rich in thank offerings.

One of the first records is that of a blind boy pilgrim, Thomas, who fell asleep in his church, where the saint appeared to him and restored his sight. (Dimitri can show each attitude, word and gesture of this cure.) Soon followed other and greater miracles, till S. Spiridione was recognised as the undoubted patron and faithful protector of all the island.

The casket of S. Spiridione rests in a richly wrought silver sarcophagus within the shrine of his church ; and the very magnificent and varied lamps of gold and silver which hang from the church roof testify to a wide appreciation of the saintly powers. For these lamps have come from Venice and even from Turkey, as thank-offerings for help given or, in some cases, as propitiations for offences against the saintly power. They are splendidly wrought, unsparing in weight and workmanship. Other treasures there are, too, not usually shown : a chalice ascribed to Cellini, massive gold altar vessels and censers of exquisite Venetian craftsmanship, and strange old holy cloths and rich vestments.

Four times in the year the casket of the saint is brought out to make procession round the town, on the anniversaries of those days when he saved Corfu from Turks, from plague, and from famine. And on his festa, which corresponds to our Christmas Eve, and at Easter, this casket of gold and glass, jewel-hung, is placed on a silver throne in the church, where for three days and two nights the body receives the homage of the crowd.

The guns of the fort officially salute each exit and entrance of the saint, and not the most modern of Corfiotes but has for him a profound respect.

An Artist in Corfu

We attended the service of the emergence of the saint on his festa. A dense crowd packed the church to its very screen, and the high civil and military officials on duty barely kept space for the entry of the priests. By Papa Boulgari's kindness we were permitted to ascend the winding wall-stair to the high pulpit, and peeping there behind its curtain we saw and heard the whole service from among the silver lamps and towering candles.

The choir priests wear vestments of cloth-of-silver and blue : beautiful things ; the bearers of the casket wear old-gold, and the Archbishop has very elaborate vestments of red and gold, to which his high black-veiled hat is a severe foil.

Before the emergence there is a long and great-sounding service of intercession, intoned and chanted by several solo priests, with vibrating responses of base chords from the unaccompanied men's voices of the choir. A very ancient-sounding feeling of worship is in it, rising at times to an almost visible heart-throb at the movement of repeated crossings.

The service culminates with the bringing out from the shrine of the holy body, which enters through the centre door of the screen, very carefully borne in its upright casket of gold and glass, and is placed securely in the silver canopied throne before the door of the shrine.

Trumpets, and the guns of the fort, and a joyous welcome from choir and church greet its advent.

Procession of Palm Sunday

But unfortunately a military band is in waiting in the gallery, and now the fine old service is incongruously marred by the blare of a marching tune. The crowd breaks forward to kiss the holy casket, and the service is abruptly at an end.

On Palm Sunday, on Easter Eve, on a certain Sunday in August, and again in November, the saint makes his commemorative progress round the town. A very stately ceremony, to which comes every peasant within reach, to set it in proper colour and feeling.

The Procession of Palm Sunday is the finest and takes the longest route, being threatened neither with excessive heat nor wet, as the others may be. The streets literally twinkle in parts with the throng of gold-hung women, their festa garb aflame in the sunshine, and the gathering of the varied costumes—and marvellous headdressing—from the different districts is most interesting.

The long route of Palm Sunday takes about three hours, as there are halts at various stations for prayers, and at the Palace a special blessing for any of the Royal family who may be present.

The procession is led by many devotees in blue cassocks, bearing, for their saint, very beautiful old gilt Venetian lanterns on long poles, enormous banners of crimson, gold-edged and tasselled, and rows of huge candles, crowned with gold and wreathed with gay ribbon streamers, each candle in its leather baldric making a strong man's burden with frequent changes.

Preceded by these amiable and somewhat irregular participants come the bands of the old and new Philharmonica (instituted when an English Governor refused the customary loan of his band for the honouring of the saint). With their plumed and brassy helmets they have quite a martial air, and they are followed by a guard of honour.

Then open lines of soldiers flank the stately advance of the old priests ; bearded men in high black hats and a most beautiful array of vestments. Except for the silver-and-blue of S. Spiridione's choir, each robe is unique, and must have descended from the far middle ages : yellow brocade with roses, emerald hemmed with gold, purple and mauve and red and maize and every rich and mellow colour one could desire straggling gently down the street in the sunshine. At last, at the back of his open files of priests, comes the old Archbishop, mitred, and in all his symbolism of vestment. With him comes a silence on the crowd, and the pulse of hands fluttering at the sign of the cross.

For immediately after the Archbishop and a chanting priest is the saint himself, borne by six sailors, under an old rich canopy of crimson and gold, supported by six silver poles and six priests.

Around are more of the great scarved and shining headed candles ; and the movement of the sign of the cross, and the silence, pass on with the progress of the saint.

It is an open and wholly genuine profession of faith,

and I think no Corfiote would venture to discredit either S. Spiridione's great and special protection of Corfu, or even the numberless smaller miracles attributed to him.

I know one man at the present day, who fled to Italy at the hint of a rebellion in distant Athens, and who is regularly ill with nervousness at election times, but who firmly and fearlessly trusts that the saint will preserve him and the rest of Corfu from the surrounding cholera.

For is it not history, dated and signed and sealed, that there were besieging Turks, but the saint kept Corfu inviolate when all Greece went under ; that there was famine, and the saint brought them ships of food ; and that plague and cholera were likewise stayed by his holy power ?

According to tradition, the procession of Easter Eve was the first and oldest, and the exact date of its institution is unknown ; but it was confirmed by a decree from Venice in 1753. Its occasion was a terrible famine which threatened all Corfu with starvation. But on Easter Eve grain ships came to port and saved the island, giving it true cause for a most joyous Easter. These ships had been destined for other ports, but the saint appeared to the captains and induced them to change their course for Corfu, where they would sell all their cargo most profitably. As the Venetians erected public granaries in 1553, it is surmised that this miracle occurred at that date or previously. The Easter Eve procession is not so fine a spectacle as the others, for it is in mourning for the dead Christ.

The great Palm Sunday procession is really the finest, and it comes next in order of antiquity.

In 1629 a deadly plague swept Italy and the Ionian Islands, threatening Corfu, during the months of October and November, and arriving, it is surmised, with some Turkish rugs on Christmas Eve. In spite of all precautions the plague spread rapidly and fatal cases occurred daily. So all the inhabitants came for succour to the shrine of the saint, and with tears besought his help ; and the historian of Corfu, Marmora, living at that time, relates that most of those attacked by the disease saw the saint appear to them in a dream, promising them deliverance and health, whereupon they were suddenly restored. Marmora also states that so long as the disease still prevailed in the town, a light as of a small lamp hovered at night over the tower of the church of S. Spiridione and was constantly observed by the sentinels of the fortress. By Palm Sunday the plague had vanished from Corfu ; and ever since, the anniversary of the deliverance has been celebrated most splendidly, the procession taking place by decree of the Venetian governors, in answer to a petition from the Syndicate of Corfu.

In 1673 plague or cholera again visited the island, and again S. Spiridione was petitioned for its banishment. He prevailed first on July 13th, the anniversary of the miracle of blind Thomas, when " behold, there happened a second miracle : the pestilence ceased, as if in the twinkling of an eye ; men and women, already half dead, were all of a sudden no longer sick." But the plague returned later in the year, and so it was not till the first Sunday in November that the island was finally freed from it, and it is on this date that the thanksgiving procession takes place.

The last great miracle was not against the forces of nature but of man. Here it is, translated from the Legendary of S. Spiridione : " The last miracle, which took place in our days and before our very eyes, is indeed wonderful to relate and most worthy of admiration. For in this present year, 1716, on the 24th June, the godless Hagarites (Turks) made a furious attack, both by land and sea, and threatened our town of Corfu with destruction, so that all the faithful reverently took refuge in prayer to the Almighty Lord and Protector ; and verily they did not fail in their entreaty ; since suddenly and contrary to all reason and expectation, the besieging enemy vanished like lightning, turned to sudden flight on the eleventh of August, not being pursued at the time except perhaps by the invisible power of God our Saviour, in answer to the powerful entreaties of the Saint. On account of this, in grateful reverence, our God-preserved aristocracy immediately sent a lamp, chased in silver, with many lights, to the sacred shrine of the saint, and determined in common council to ordain a yearly procession with the sacred body on the day on which

the deliverance took place, and, moreover, that 150
silver coins should be distributed to the poor by the
Archbishop (Roman Catholic) and the first priest,
Protopappos (Greek) of the town."

In the Life of S. Spiridione there is the following
account of the actual circumstances of the Turkish
rout. " . . . the infidel hordes suddenly appeared
before the town, and besieged it by land and by sea.
From the beginning of the war they oppressed the
town and the citizens with fire and sword, and after
fifty days, during which many fierce battles were
fought, the barbarians resolved to concentrate their
forces upon the town of Corfu. Then all the faithful
besought the help of the saint, day and night, with
tears and groanings. Whereupon while the army of
the Hagarites was attacking the citadel, a terrible
destruction and scattering of their forces was brought
about through the intercession of the saint ; upon this,
the barbarians breathed still greater vengeance and
inhuman cruelty, threatening the city with another
attack and the dire calamities of captivity and death.
The entreaties, however, and prayers of the faithful
did not cease, as in humble reverence they called upon
the protection and assistance of their common father,
nor did this their prayer remain unheard. For while
the Corfiotes were awaiting wholesale destruction by
the barbarians—at early dawn one morning there appeared to the enemy our great father Spiridione, with
a mighty heavenly host, holding in his right hand a

sword flashing lightning, and furiously pursuing them. The Ottoman soldiers, on seeing such a wonderful vision, turned suddenly to flight, and in their panic, from fear of being wounded by an invisible enemy, fell over one another in great confusion. So they fled and were destroyed by their fear, without enemy, or fire, or sword, or anything else pursuing them—through the invincible power of our Lord God, on the fervent intercession of the wonder-working S. Spiridione. And when the infantry and cavalry retreated, the fleet also took its departure and thus Corfu was left free. So, on the morning when the citizens were expecting the usual fighting, they beheld everything silent and quiet. Whereupon they went, full of curiosity, into the tents of the enemy, and there beholding the miracle that had been performed, they leapt with joy and rejoiced at the new and wonderful state of affairs, as not only did they see the Ishmaelites put to flight, but they also found all their belongings left behind as booty. And those who were fleeing openly confessed that they had been turned into sudden flight by a monk, that is to say, S. Spiridione, who had appeared in the air with a glorious heavenly host. Then all gladly and reverently repaired to the saint's church, glorifying God, and giving thanks to the saint." *

So the last procession of S. Spiridione was instituted, on August 11th, in commemoration of this miracle on

* From "Saint Spiridione, Patron Saint of Corfu, and the processions held in his honour." (L. Brokinis. Translated by A. S. Dawes.)

that date. This was the Turks' last great assault on Christendom. Corfu, which had so long held out as the last outpost against the Moslem flood, turned back the tide. Christ and Spiridione triumphed.

Dimitri's editions of these miracles are really delightful, though hardly authentic in detail perhaps. But he gives each word and gesture of the saint's encounter with the cholera, as of a happening of this week; till one almost sees the discomfited disease fleeing back to Italy in the form of a black cat.

His version of the fast of the Madonna, in broad Venetian patois, is also very charming and graphic. There is a certain fortnight at the end of August which is kept a more strict fast than any other in the year. "And the reason for this, Signorina, is that once Christ got very very vexed with the world, so that he was just going to destroy it a second time (for you know it was destroyed once ; the old pieces are underneath Corfu ; if you dig in the town you will find them). But Mamma was grieved at this and said : There then, leave it, leave it, my dear ; and she fasted and prayed very hard for a fortnight, and so she persuaded the Christ to leave the world unbroken. And so we must certainly keep this fast in honour of the Virgin, you see Signorina."

May Corfu long be happy in such unquestioning faith.

CHAPTER XI

Little Journeys

THE hireling carriage—*carozza*—is the universal means of going about in Corfu. Even peasants go shares, many shares, in the village carrozze when travelling any considerable distance; and the Court officials in attendance on any royal visitors must be content with the same mode of conveyance, for there is no other. Cycling, however, is both possible and pleasant for those who do not mind the interruptions of long hills and can manage their own repairing. The English legacy of good roads is very fairly maintained, and by it every district may be visited.

The only, but important, difficulty is that of accommodation. A stranger in Corfu would be limited to his day's capacity for riding; for except for a tiny German guest-house at Gastouri there are no possible lodgings outside the town, and though the island is not large its mountainous formation and winding ways forbid any speedy review of its charms.

For any one with friends in the island this difficulty hardly exists, however, for every little estate has its little country house—the properties of all the island are interwoven by generations of marriage portions and subdivisions—and though it is difficult for a stranger to hire a house, it is probable that a friendly loan of

185

one will be offered in any district we would explore. These little cottages or villas stand empty, as a rule, for the greater part of the year, and though some are well tended and cared for by their owners, they are as a rule allowed to fall into sad disrepair ; neglected shrines sometimes for fine old bits of despised Venetian handiwork, long banished from the Victorian drawing-rooms in town.

My first little journey in Corfu was during the Easter holidays, when we went over the back of the Spartile range to explore the northern circle of the island. This is probably the most primitive portion of Corfu, for the mountain barrier isolates it from sea to sea and all communications with town and the rest of the island must either be laboriously by pass, or circuitously by boat.

Like nearly every road in Corfu, ours was beautiful all the way. Westward from town, for some miles it skirts at shore level the lovely bay of Govino, the bay which cuts the island to within ten miles of the western sea ; then still westward we passed inland through pastoral olive-covered land and little rocky valleys, rising gradually to the long hillside village of Skripero. Resting at a wayside café here we had the fortune to be found by friends going into the country for the holidays, and, as we were likewise fortunate in finding boys capable of pushing bicycles, we took the pass of Pantaleone* in their carozza luxuriously. This

---

* Hagios Panteleïmon.

Dust and Hospitality

is the highest road pass on the island, 1040 feet. It is the usual arrangement of severe zig-zags; on the summit there is a magnificent view back over all the southern portion of the island, the Straits, and the end-less chains of Albanian mountains. We reached the summit at sunset, and the town lay in the Straits like an inlaid jewel of gold.

We hastened from the bitter wind, stumbled in the dusk down a very indifferent track, and did not reach our borrowed home at Ali Matadis until dark. It is a village of extreme poverty and unsophistication. Kindly natives carried our cycles and steered ourselves down and up the uncouth causeways to a house that was in all ways correspondent to its surroundings. An ancient caretaker met us in the court, but though pre-vised of our coming, he had thought no preparation necessary, and when we got out a candle and went upstairs (the house was over its magazine in the usual way), we found it unvisited and untouched since the vintage. The dust of six months was undisturbed on its crumbling relics of furniture. But undisturbed *we* were not, for from the time we entered we were ceaselessly tormented with fleas—why they cannot go on living on the dust is always a mystery—they were so voracious that even a peasant whom I wished to sketch could not sit still, and a peasant usually ignores fleas.

They certainly took toll on our holiday, but except for them it was quite perfect.

An Artist in Corfu

We lit candles, swept off the thick of the dust, and explored for bedding. (The beds were damper than one could have imagined possible, but this apparently does not matter when one is camping.) Margariti meanwhile prepared supper, for we were quite tired and hungry. The primitive village could produce for us nothing but bread and cheese (and lamb of course on Easter Day), but we had brought a provident store of butter, cake, chocolate, many hard-boiled eggs, and some rice and coffee, and on these we lived very happily, though our last dinner was reduced to bread and butter, cheese and chocolate. The primitive village could not even produce charcoal, so that Margariti's attempts at cooking were enhanced by the acid flavour of wood smoke. Margariti was a canny old man, but too obviously a tender of sheep; and I was sorry that I happened to see him taking his supper off our loaf.

Ali Matadis perches high on the northern side of Spartile range : so barren a hillside that one wonders how the village exists at all, and can hardly be indignant at its starved dogs. The people are fine in type, though without any of the opulence of the Gastouri belles. The views are wonderful. Beyond the narrow northern Straits, the towering white peaks run sheer down into the sea, and north-west of the undulating lowlands of Corfu a pretty group of islets dots the sea. Of these, one, Fano, is called Calypso's isle, and another is the ship of Ulysses in full sail, undeniably " that winged pinnace " . . . " The God arrests her with a sudden stroke, And roots her down an everlasting rock," here, and not at Pontikonisi.

Our first expedition was up over the north-western shoulder of Spartile and down its most abrupt termination to the sea. It was an entrancing walk, though rough on untrained feet. We hired a small bearer, aged about twelve, who cheerfully bore a substantial sack of lunch and sketching kit by a rope on his thinly clad shoulder, and skipped barefoot far in advance of our labouring steps.

We went up the usual kind of watercourse pathway, and then down the coast end equally stonily till our knees ached, while like Tom over Vendale, we thought we could have thrown stones into the marvellous sea so far below. It is even more marvellous here than round the rest of Corfu, for the coast is all fretted and cut into tiny bays and points and islets and peninsulas, and about them the clear deep water lies, in colours that not poets could find name for.

It is not like any other sea—perhaps they are the colours of the thoughts of its God that still move it so wonderfully.

Half-way down to the sea we rested at Lakones, and there the village acquaintance, who always appeared so opportunely in our wanderings, added fruit and wine to our luggage, and we were allowed to proceed. We had still a great depth to go; indeed the sea seemed no nearer yet, for all our descent. We went almost straight now, down a fine cleft or gorge, with water the colour of gems and enamels and flowers inset below us, and great tufts of pure gold broom hung in the crags beside. Cushions of Virginian stock and cystus lay about our rocky paths, and it was on this walk that I found a score of flowers for my flower-diary, though I hardly left the most direct way or had time to linger on it.

On the rock most directly below us, and connected only by a shallow neck with the mainland, stands the old monastery of Paleokastrizza, surmised the site of an ancient fort, and most deservedly one of Corfu's show places. We joined the main road from town about half a mile from the shore. It was hot, we missed the mountain air, and found the little climb to the monastery absurdly laborious. I wish you could see it, the primitive peaceful place, with its white-washed vine-trellised courts and unpretentious buildings. Towards the shore it is all lapped in olives and almond blossom ; westward its walls hold on to cliffs that drop sheer to the waves.

As we climbed the road among the olives, round a corner into the blazing sun, we came upon a flock of sheep, in their midst a thin black figure, unshorn beard and head, and the youngest lamb on his shoulders.

In later visits I made acquaintance with one or two of the monks and found them as kindly and hospitable as the rest of the Corfiotes, and their simplicity apparently quite untouched by the stream of spring visitors. They farm their lands, and busy themselves about their oil-

PALEOKASTRIZZA.

making with their skirts kilted up, and probably they differ very slightly from their peasant neighbours. But it is a place of peace.

There is a large church and a pillared court of vines, and a row of massive arched ways to the cells of the brethren over the magazines.

We had an audience with the abbot, a venerable person with wrinkles ingrained black, who inhabits two cupboard-sized chambers, their walls covered with fine old gold and silver ikons, and modern prints and photographs. The Kaiser had interviewed him only a few days before.

The beautiful old church plate—great silver lamps, etc.—was all huddled in a box. Peasants never can understand damagable property it seems.

After lunch, kindly supplemented by the monks, we went down to the shore of the nearest bay and watched the live sea, what time the untiring boy gamboled and threw stones. Rested and refreshed we climbed the gorge to Lakones, but there we mutinied. The boy went gaily up over the mountain with his sack, but we chose the northwards road with its more gradual climb round the mountain's end. Lakones was horrible, unsightly with Easter lamb, but we were constrained to refreshment in the midst ; the very dustiest room I ever saw, the Town Hall I believe it was. This northwards road is on the way to St. Angelo, and we had a fine view of that crag-fast ruin beyond a sea-deep gorge. It is so very very old that it has forgotten the present, and lives and dreams among its days of young romance.

Leaving the steep coastward mountain-side we passed inland through most park-like country and then gradually up on to the broad back of Spartile again—with sunset over the whole length of it ; and so back to Margariti's wood-flavoured supper at the darkening.

On another day, equally fine and hot, we had a very pleasant tour towards the north coast. Our cycles were carried down the stepped and cobbled causeway to the more civilised village of Arkadades, and from there we strayed delightfully along the very curly roads that lead down to the northern lowlands. The views were ever changing as we circled among the little irregular hills and ridges, and there was no lack of excitement riding through villages whose dogs were new to bicycles and their hilly roads unsurfaced.

It was Easter Sunday, and we were invited to lunch at Karusades, but could hardly escape delay from another hospitable friend who waylaid us at his house in a dear little fertile plain, with a real permanent river, and a mill not far away.

At one place our road was glorified for half a mile or more by a fringe of asphodel a yard high and several yards deep, shining most radiantly.

Our hosts at Karusades were of the small number who live permanently in their country home, and we found it an interesting old place, quite repaying our particularly long and hot climb. There are about it

Hospitality

still hints of its fortified past. Its high-walled gardens
stand above the village, and its higher walled courts
above the gardens. As our approach had not been
noticed we stood for some time quite helplessly without
the walls. But once admitted, we found the patriarchal household as kindly hospitable as any in Corfu.
The house rambled along in the midst and above its
strong old courtyards in a desultory way, having from
time to time amiably accommodated itself to the
patriarchal needs. The gardens were well kept, and
very charming with their spring flowers ; the house
was—not so well kept ; the inhabitants—well, no
Corfiote but a peasant will ever put on a new garment in the country, and though it was Easter
Sunday the patriarchs and their descendants did not
compete with the Easter costumes of their peasants.

We parted from these kind hosts with many delays
and armfuls of fragrant blossoms, after watching the
village dance. Enjoying the cooler ride down, we
were again constrained to pause at the friends' in the
plain. We were refreshed with coffee, of course, and
they insisted on escorting us home, in turn, in the
queerest little pony trap, funnier and crookeder even
than Babatzo's. We enjoyed the arrangement of
sunset lighting on this side of the mountain, new to us,
and the dusk was lovely too, on the high road we
followed along the steep side of it, by giant cypresses
and sleepy hamlets, through the blessed silence, with
a murmur of the legends of Spiridione on our ears.

An Artist in Corfu

We left our bicycles at Arkadades for the morrow, and stumbled up the half-mile or so of causeway as well as we could ; in the dusk, as usual, before we got back to Margariti and his wood-smoked provision.

The villages we passed had all been dancing ; but it was on Monday that we chanced on the best dances, and saw, I think, on the whole, the most wonderful country. Among all the enchanting beauties of Corfu that day stands alone, having for sole rival the day of our later pilgrimage to Castelangelo.

Having packed away the borrowed house for another long sleep, by nine o'clock on Monday morning we started downhill for our cycles : I found mine with a broken brake, but fortunately also in the next village a genius who mended it, and so wound back to our friends in the plain. Here hospitality was only satisfied by our pausing for several hours while a simple but excellent feast was prepared and eaten. This little home was a great contrast to the straggling household of yesterday. A tiny but very well kept house standing simply among garden and farm buildings beside the road, very primitive but cared for and compact. In these days it is quite strange to come on such entirely isolated lives as these, in the winter seeing no one, at other seasons equally isolated, but for a very occasional visit to town. Quite happy, with their powder-flask of gourd, and their shot-horn of bamboo, their home-grown fare and home-made appliances.

Our friends again escorted us on our way, taking E.

Roadside Diversions

in the comical pony cart right to the farther side of
the mountains. It was sunsetting ere we parted ;
and then the dogged little pony Fly was to bring them
home again over that tremendous range.

We went back on our tracks from the little house
as far as the mill, then turned leftwards to approach
the mountain chain at Sokraki, further east than at
Pantaleone. The road meandered with persistence
and great beauty, and climbed by very slow gradations
from the full luxuriance of olives and plains to the
wildest rocky valleys. It was a glorious day of sunshine
and fresh wind, and among the grey and golden rocks
the olive-trees hung above us like pure silver against
the intense blue of the sky. I have never felt anything
more exhilarating and joyous than the air that day,
nor seen more loveliness than there was, above and
below and around the windings of that mountain road,
and stretched away over land and sea. It is strange
that the people no longer see gods in their trees and
waters and hills.

We passed through several little eagle's-nest villages,
and others hung higher still on the rocky shoulders of
the mountains. The people were all dancing, and the
twinkle of festa clothes carried from the far high
distance. How we turned and twisted about. The road
became quite hard work for pushing towards the end.
but swept in such a splendid curve of wide vista round
the mountain-side that one could not be tired. There
were all the white ranges of Albania shining marvel-

lously above the Straits. There was an organ-song of sunlight going up from the whole earth.

So we climbed for about three hours and gained the head of our pass at the village of Sokraki, where we longed to stay awhile, but after the heat of the ascent the knife-edged wind soon drove us on. We took a chilly shelter meanwhile in a house over the village street, and watched the finest dancing I have seen in Corfu.

The women's dresses were rich and fine, and their rhythmic and unchanging accompaniment was all proper. But the men, the soloists always in these dances—on the rough village street, in socks or Turkish slippers—danced as I thought only professionals in a finely trained ballet could do; with flying bounds across the circle of dancing; with intricate steps and twirlings in the air; and with a perfect flexibility and lightness that one could hardly realise was quite untrained.

The cold drove us reluctantly on, down the very steepest mountain-side that a road could hang on. Our way lay like a knotted string below us, so tightly curled we could see it only in parts ; and it had horrible giddy corners with the surface off too.

We had seen so much, near and far, in our climbing and crossing, that when we came down to the asphodel levels the plant seemed like a friend long unseen. We passed along the big village town of Korakiana, important enough to support two or three dances, and after

An Expedition to the South

another mile or two, said good-bye to our friends, who were going to return by Skripero and Pantaleone. In clear gold sunset and pansy dusk we circled the bay of Ypso, felt like returned wanderers along our familiar Gastouri road, and climbed the gorge short-cut by moonlight and the first fireflies of the season. We arrived about nine o'clock to find the servants were going to bed, having *forgotten* we were returning, and there was neither food nor fire prepared for us. Horrid anti-climax! but the ecstasy of the day outlasted it.

Our next expedition was at Whitsuntide, June 13th, and already hot weather, so we started about five o'clock in the afternoon. We were going southwards this time, and our first toil was to get up the wearisome hill to Santi Deka—our opposite neighbouring village that looks so near, on its mountain side, and has such a depth between. Fortunately, though it was festa, we managed to secure a boy for our laden bicycles, so had not to face the endless zig-zags of the main road. There are (I need hardly say so, perhaps!) fine views from the mountain-side, and Gastouri would be perfect from here if the excessive bulk of the Achilleion and its annexe did not so disturb the picture.

From S. Deka village the road climbs more gently towards Stavro, and then passes south-west between the two mountains and comes out very high over a long plain stretching southward to the sea. It is worth some toil to come through here to the west at sunset time, and this road has always favoured me with some

197

particular manifestation; a wedding procession,—a bringing home of dowry,—or some gay enhancement of its charms.

For this my first sight it gave me a blaze of most golden sunset light flat on to the precipitous mountain side; and in its full glory the whole homebound population of the village, party after party, strung along the cliff in colour like flame above the blue valley shadows. A goodly sight to see.

We ran down by gentle slopes through several miles of glorious sunset into the plain. Peaks and pyramids of hill, with here and there a touch of the sea between, cut up into the glowing sky; and at earliest dusk the full moon rose, while we went on southward to the shore.

Perhaps olives look best by moonlight; I am not sure.—The lovely oft-enchanted trees!

When we came near the sea there were flat spaces of sands and wide lagoons: strange they seemed in craggy Corfu. We turned eastward for a mile or two and presently came to the foot of a hill on our left, leading up into a mystery of olives and moonlight. There was no village; the few cottages we had passed had all been deep asleep. There was no one to wheel our bicycles! Had we known how far and steep and stony was the road, I think we would have slept by the way-side. But we went on and on in hope, and by about ten o'clock reached the high village of Khlomos, were guided to our charming borrowed house, and all our toils repaid by Corfu's delightful trick of an unanticipated and glorious view. The house lies seaward from the village, at the very corner of that coned hill in the sickle's bend. The windows of my room looked north and east. Ah, the loveliest Straits, in that Corfiote moonlight that has no black in it ! Away to the north the lights of forts and town twinkled, and even Spartile beyond was faintly visible in that radiant atmosphere.

The night was so fresh up there, and the morning glorious. Northwards our mountain falls almost precipitously towards the sea; but eastward rolls in olive-clad hills to the slender exquisite curve of the sickle point.

Southward, the open sea, and little Paxos and Antipaxos.

Our borrowed house was beautifully kept for an attentive master ; had even an excellent cook caretaker, and of necessities lacked only—a road, and water ! There was no way of approach but the vague and rocky foot-ways about the backs of village huts. And all water had to be carried from a distance on donkeyback. So that a young attempt at an orchard was a barren and piteous sight, though the courtyard was beautiful with oleanders in fullest flower and scent.

The village ran further up the mountain, a most unspoilt and picturesque place of steep ways and cheerful simplicity. It had not the pinched and barbaric pearance of Ali Metadis,—possibly a result of a partly resident landlord,—and the people were charming and most friendly.

I had hardly penetrated far, on the Whitsunday

morning, and was sketching, sorely afflicted with dust and too warmly interested natives, in a narrow and ancient alley, when a little procession of fiddler and priest passed gaily down, and I learned that I would see my first village wedding in this delightful place.

The wedding occupied us nearly the whole day, but we took a rest in the middle, for it was very hot.

First we were led to the house of the bride, where strong hands dragged us through the waiting crowd, up the packed staircase to the upper room. Here we were introduced as honoured guests to see the counting of the dowry.

In order that there may be no after disputes and recriminations, the stipulated dower is catalogued and read from a list by the bride's father, and as each item is named it is picked up by one of the bride's maids and carried out on her head : mattresses, linen, heaps of blue cotton skirts, aprons, kerchiefs, furniture, and festa clothes with their gayest side displayed. It is a brave show, and then when all is counted the fiddler heads the excited and chattering procession up the steep ways (not even cobbled here—just worn mountain side) to the new home higher in the village. Here many hands quickly set in order the furniture, pack away the clothing, and prepare the bridal bed.

At this point we withdrew for lunch interval, and when we returned there had been a feast, and the bride was already decked for the church. We were again elevated through the crowd, and somehow inserted in

A Wedding

the bride's tiny inner chamber. It was absolutely packed with women, and there was much talking and laughing, while the bonny young bride sat rather overcome and very still in the midst; for she would court bad luck by moving before her father came to lead her away. A wild old crone had to reiterate many times for our admiration and her glory that it was she who had tired the head of the bride. The result was truly brilliant and striking; completed with a huge wreath of braids, tinsels and flowers. But the fine regular features carried it all easily.

Presently came in father and brother and led out the bride; and they and all the principals, with a queue of bridesmaids holding hands or handkerchiefs, danced several circles very solemnly in the village street, before following the indispensable fiddler in a long procession up to the church. The women here are very handsome and their dresses most sumptuous, so that all these little processions filtering about the village were delightful to watch.

We were given " stalls " in Church, and were glad enough of their support, for it was very hot and crowded, and the service rather long, as most of the Greek services are.

But how beautiful in sound—the numerous litanies and their chanted responses, and the long great-sounding prayers! Four peasants in the stalls sang in solo or in harmonies, taking up their parts from the beckoning of the priest. I am told that much of the village church music is handed on orally, and I do not think these men had any printed books. The marriage service includes an exchange of rings, and three inter-changings of the gold and silver wreaths which the best man places on the heads of bride and bridegroom. Finally there is a little procession round inside the church, with many pauses for blessing. Then rice is thrown, both in church and from the wayside windows and stairways, as the bride is led home, and every one eats sugared almonds. And, at home, the newly wed sit and receive congratulations, and little gifts of money cast into the bride's lap, and other presents.

And then the untiring people dance for hours.

It was then we came away, feeling rather sated with peasants, and realised we had no change of raiment after the very hot and dusty crowd. We went and sat on the vine terraces over the sea. The mountains opposite were of dim and tawny velvet, and over them presently came a red moon in the dusk.

Next day a charming bride-to-be donned all her wedding finery—secretly, for fear of village mocking—that I might sketch her. She came escorted by her betrothed and a party of friends and stood for several hours. And the whole party was so grieved at the idea of any remuneration, that it had to be discreetly pressed as a wedding-present! Delightful village!

When we bade it farewell in the late afternoon, about a third of the inhabitants must have rushed to shake our hands, and give us good wishes.

CHAPTER XII

A Second Chapter of Journeys

IT was at the end of January that E. and I adventured, with little Lenne, the maid, and a carozza full of blankets and provender, to a village in the west. Winter weather had been very unsettled, but Corfu relents so often and so swiftly that we started full of hopes. The village of Doukades is about three hours from town. (Observe, we cannot measure by accurate distance in the south, so that to visit a friend we might describe it a drive as of two and a half hours, while we could tack on an extra hour if we did not wish to go. This is so convenient.)

For Doukades, we leave the Skripero road on our right where it turns to the hills, keeping on the main road to Paleokastrizza for a few miles further. Doukades is half a mile, maybe, above the road, tucked away under an eastward-facing crag of Spartile; and when we arrived just after sunset the village was only a blur of almond blossom and wood smoke beneath the long garden-terraces of our borrowed house. The great wall of Spartile cut down our view on the north; there were a few touches of Straits in the distance, and over them the long snows of Epiros, dun in the twilight, with a last finger of the sun among their clouds.

The garden terraces were heavy with oranges,

citrons and mandarins. It was a dear little house. It was very cold. There was a fireplace (*that* we had ascertained before coming) ; but it smoked from first to last, most bitterly.

Next morning we tied ourselves up firmly and in a great gale strove up the steep old footway that leads over the mountains to Ali Matadis and district. We crawled about on top, meeting a few wind-bent peasants, the women in curious open-necked shifts and open-fronted coats. We went back and peeped over the giant cliffs that crest the range westward to the sea— a sheer perpendicular wall, scored with deep chimneys and eaten into caves at the base.

Later in the day we climbed along below the cliffs, by the veriest goat-tracks, and managed to reach one or two of these caves. Some of them are fitted with hurdles, and are reputed to shelter as many as 1,000 sheep. In one were marks of a fire, and a tin can caught the roof-drippings. We saw no other furniture. But E. in her wanderings met a wild shepherd who told her he lived there. A highly unclean person, one would gather, though it sounds all right at a distance.

We had been full of plans of what we would do from Doukades, but the rain quenched them with steady persistence. But our second day appeared shining gloriously, and with painting kit and no precautions we set forth for Paleokastrizza, four or five miles down the main road below. It was a jewel of a morning, and we came upon that sea all foaming, malachite green in its rocky bays, with cliff shadows on it of deep amethyst. We stood for long entranced, and little Lenne, whom we could not leave alone in a strange village, was quite excited, and cast stones down into the milky spurts against the rocks. The road is of very wonderful beauty all the way.

When we reached the monastery it began to rain very gently; while we essayed to lunch off eggs that were not hard-boiled it rained harder; so after an hour or two of patience in the long guest chamber over the waves we decided to start homewards in Corfu's special semi-tropical rain. Lenne was in her festa clothes, the new blue velvet jacket that had been her joy since Christmas. However, she just took off one of her numerous thick cotton skirts and wrapped it over her head; and when the sun came out with an exasperating smile about three-quarters of an hour after, she was drier than we in our sodden tweeds.

Then we sat indoors for days while it roared with rain. When there was a lull, we sallied out and got wet, and returned again to the smoky fire; and on two days I managed to seize some pleasant hours of sketching alone at Paleokastrizza. But we had waited till the utmost limit of holiday ere the day arrived for which we were hoping—for which, in fact, we had come to Doukades.

It was on February 7th, and a very perfect day, that we set out for Castleangelo. We had meant to do this expedition in state, *i.e.*, with Spiro and donkeys;

but after the long storm every inhabitant and every donkey was busy at the olive gathering, so perforce we went alone (Lenne had made friends in the village, and was chaperoned in our absence by Marina, the wife of Spiro).

We went for a mile or two down the Paleokastrizza road : the grey-shaded road, where wild figures evolve silent as nature-spirits from wayside olives, and vast fragments of rock lie scattered from the great cliffs that wall the northern heavens. Then up to the right where the cliffs bend back, we cut the long windings at a causeway which we hoped was old as the crusaders, and slowly and admiringly climbed to Lakones.

On that blue and glorious day Lakones was lost in almond blossom. It floated like a dazzling cloud above us and was just as radiant against the jade-green bays and bluer depths of sea below. The red-tiled roofs had scarce a note to say through it. The whole village blossomed against the mountain side.

Behind us our own mountains of the south were steeped in blue, were blue as the sea, and far over in the east Albania shone with newest snow. Verily an entrancing world. We went straight through Lakones to the north, and passed round the deep and shadowy gorge beyond which hangs, like the fortress of a dream, St. Angelo over the sea. By a side road we came to Krini, over against our fortress, and here a nasty un-romantic fact was intruded on us; for Spiro had assured us we could buy provision for lunch at Krini, and unfortunately we had more than half believed him. And Krini, like the rest of Corfu, was away olive-picking with every available hand, its sole representatives at home, three small and useless children! No shop or cottage was open, we could not even beg or steal bread, and so fared onward with unplenished scrip.

There is no road or possibility of a road to St. Angelo.

An isolated cone, a rocky needle, shoots a sheer thousand feet from the sea, and about its head the walls of St. Angelo are fast bound like a diadem. It is only a little place, and there is not much of it left, but the wonder and the beauty of it are like nothing else.

From Krini a steep and rocky descent leads to the narrow neck which joins the cone at about half its height, and an even steeper ascent zig-zags up to the crumbled walls far above in the blue air. A donkey could do the ascent, a led horse might manage the lower part, but I should not like to try it on a very windy day.

The track was so faded that we climbed precariously round under the walls to the seaward face of the cone before we were sure we had lost it. There was something rather terrible about the silent glittering water, so very far and directly below, and I crawled ignominiously back, while E. scaled the walls. About the entrance on the landward side a triple line of defence is vaguely seen, though only the inmost wall remains. The gate of the second wall is a mere postern for size, and on so steep a rock-stairway that one wonders what fanatics dared attempt it.

The walls literally hang round the cone, and within their narrow bounds we are told 3,000 refugees huddled for that terrible siege of the Turks. Three thousand, and parched, no doubt, and scorched by the fierce August sun.

Now the buildings are crumbled to earth again, and grass clothes all the rocky slopes, and an old woman with a few sheep moves slowly across, come up to tend the lamp of a tiny peasant chapel which rises over the ruins of Franks and Venetians.

It is said that the place takes its name from Michael the bastard, Despot of Epiros, and thorn in the flesh of the western masters of Greece in the years of the fourth Crusade. Let us certainly have Michael the Despot here too,—the place is saturated with story and romance.

There is no wall on the north. We crawled to the edge and put our heads over and looked long at the big slow rollers coming in along the shore, so very far below that they were no larger than ripples, and sent us up only a sleepy murmur. A triumphant spear of rock comes through here above all the building. It is on the north-west corner, and in it have been laid— what great chiefs and stern fighters? There some were cradled, for the stone is cut, coffined in the form of a man, there, and by the chapel too.

We found some shade, and lunched off hard-boiled

eggs and chocolate, thanks to our confidence in Spiro. However, it was not such a "revolting mixture" as Stevenson's bologna sausage, chocolate and brandy ; also I think it was raining on Stevenson,* while we had just to sit and marvel at the beauty of the world. The sea was of unimaginable blue and silver, and everything at its springtime best.

Very reluctantly we came away, skirting Krini by a sylvan byway. And about three o'clock fell voraciously on bread and cheese at Lakones. We ate in the street ; it was cleaner than the shop. But they brought us a table and stools, and then a tablecloth, and by my faith, napkins, too ! And the assembled parliament into which we had walked all melted away to a civil distance from our meal.

A young man wished to attend us as interpreter, for he had been in San Francisco for some years. He knew remarkably little American, though he had been in a restaurant business. He had saved up to return and see his old parents, found he could not remain, and was eager to escape again. " Such a little country here, and not gentlemen ; in America, *all* gentlemen, is it not ? " There was the constant tragedy of the half-developed !

Spiro took us one day to an election for demarch (district mayor) at Skripero—a lovely walk through olives. The village was packed with voters, for it was an important centre. I hastily sketched one very

* *Travels with a Donkey.*

ragged gentleman, and considerable discussion took place in the crowd as to whether I had overpaid my model or whether he ought not to have demanded 15 drachmae (12s. 6d.) for his few minutes' posing.

Every man in Greece has both municipal and parliamentary suffrage. The country also enjoys single-chamber government. And *still* it is not Utopian.

We left Doukades in pouring rain. Little lakes by the wayside were extended to swamps, and the whole country streamed. But we had achieved S. Angelo, and nothing else mattered.

Many pleasant wanderings we had about the island on Sundays and holidays, on foot or on bicycles ; among remote and curly hill villages, or to any place indulging in a special festa or procession.

On Easter Monday the village of Viro takes its banners and ikon down to Cressida, and embarks in a procession of boats for a pilgrimage to Pontikonisi : very pretty to watch. On the festa of San Giovanni, Gastouri goes in early morning to the little chapel in the woods down the Benizza road. The priests in their vestments, the big crimson banners and ikons are the central objects in these processions, and sometimes the singing is very pleasant.

A very interesting service is the Good Friday evening procession of the burial (this is national, of course, not local). About eight o'clock we were guided to the village church by candle-light, and waited only an hour while the service was finishing. Inside, the church

was packed full, with men in the nave, and women in the porches. We were given long candles to hold, children carried smaller, according to size, but every one bore a light, and the rows of peasants inside were brilliantly lit up.

Presently a tall crucifix was carried out, and the bier, all lit with candles. The old priest carried the book of the Gospel in front, and the choirmen came singing. Behind them streamed out all the congregation and followed up the cobbled alleys of the village, the candles making a fine strange light among the dark houses. Then we came to the upper church, where there were more prayers, but not for long, and finally we watched the procession winding up among the olives to the chapel of St. Michaele, the candles blending with the fireflies among the trees.

One day we drove across by many hills and villages towards Hermones. In the Val di Ropa we put up the horses, and lunched in a garden of beautiful neglected rose-trees. Then we went afoot through some miles of olive wood vaguely tracked, and down to a miniature beach where the sand burnt our passing feet, and steeply up again to the little monastery of Myrtiotyssis. It is far remoter than Paleokastrizza, and though without the commanding and wonderful situation of the latter it is very beautiful; a little cluster of old buildings and walled gardens nested above the sea among the olives.

We lost ourselves in the woods, coming back. It was a very pleasant pilgrimage. When we returned to the rose garden we found its owner had unexpectedly arrived from town. And the awkward part of it was that our intrusion had *not* been arranged for, as we thought, and neither our large party nor the horses had any right to their agreeable quarters. The owner was very good. He rose to the occasion and heaped many lovely flowers on our confusion. It was rather a painful mistake, though, to make with a mere acquaintance.

The drive to Pelleka is one that most visitors to Corfu achieve, for the way is beautiful, and from the crag-top over the village (" conveniently reached by a carriage road ") there is a wonderfully representative view over the island. Peleka is on a conspicuous and narrow hill not far from the wonderful west coast. One overlooks its peaks and crags, its tiny bays and bold curves, far below through the olives, while eastward the whole middle reach of the island, from Spartile to tiny Kyria Ki and our mountains in the south, is spread below us ; there are rolling hills crowned with villages ; the bay, the town, and at our feet the Val di Ropa.

Being a show place, a German tourist will be found on the topmost crag, and six small but insistent children will beg. But our German lent us matches for our spirit lamp, and the children were only gently clamorous. And over the Straits it was so light and sunny that a rainbow could not have shown fairer colour. So we make no complaint of Pelleka.

Last Days

The time came when the last days in Corfu were numbered, and every hour treasured.

On one of these last days we arose early, drove into town, and set out in a little sailing boat for Kasoppa in the north.

It is supposed that Kasoppa may have been the capital of Alcinous; it is known that Nero danced before an altar there, on his way to Greece, and in later days the shrine of Our Lady of Kasoppa was a favourite with homeward faring Crusaders. So we went to see it.

It was a glorious morning, the sunny world all mirrored about us in the Straits. Our men had to row for hours across the bay, but when we reached the Straits proper we met a stiff breeze and by many long tacks made small progress. The sea was of most splendid ultramarine and white, but we began to doubt our ever attaining Kasoppa. However, by two o'clock we were put ashore in the veriest gem of a bay. Fifty yards of narrow gravel, finished by grey rocks and encircled by meadow, olive shadowed glades knee-deep in flowers, wonderful even for Corfu. The lovely pink hawkweed and its golden fellow, with a deep rose-coloured pink, were responsible for the floods and waves of alternating rose and gold. They literally hid the grass. But the blue campanula, small purple larkspur, tall fair lupin and many other flowers were only less abundant. All these against the deep blue of the ruffled sea—unforgettably lovely and of the ancient world.

An Artist in Corfu

We lunched and lingered, and then went north for about a mile to rejoin our boat at Kasoppa.

This is at the north-east corner of the island, commanding the entrance to the Straits. All that is left of the ancient capital now is a tiny sea-port hamlet, a church of the usual village type, but guarded with high walls, and on a low flat hill to the north the remains of a vast fortified enclosure, of which only the broken shell of a gatehouse, the strong line of the walls, and a few fragments of wall-towers are still standing. Inside are fields of corn and vegetables, and in the middle, what appears to be an ancient threshing floor.

Our boat danced us quickly back into the Straits, and as there were of course friends to be visited on the way, we had a very pleasant pause at Kouloura. This is a charming old fortified house just a few yards above the waves, on a rocky point from which the land runs steeply up. Cascades of geraniums fell from walls to waves, and the landing is at a most beautiful little circular basin, a tiny natural harbour, at the very gate. A handful of fishing-boats lay there, but all the village is safely inland, a steep mile or two from the shore. The old part of the house is most solidly vaulted, and has four round corner turrets; but later safer years have added verandahed rooms to catch the breezes and the vistas of the Straits. Altogether a charming place.

A wonderful twilight was over sea and twinkling town as we came across the bay, and as the breeze held fresh we were ashore by ten o'clock.

Last Days

This is the end.

My last journey in Corfu, from house to steamer, was rather typical of the island's ways. For neither baggage cart nor carrozza turned up, though we had allowed hours' margin to both. Finally the baggage was got off, just in time. We, heavily laden, at last toiled in great heat and anxiety to the village, fortunately caught a stray carriage and so caught the boat. We heard casually by the way that the carozza ordered had cast a wheel on its way.

Blessed benighted little Corfu. It is only twelve hours from Brindisi; fifty-six from London by the mail : yet most of its inhabitants have never seen a train. May it ever be preserved from casinos and their clans, a haunt for those who love natural beauty, and the peace it gives.

THE END.

CPSIA information can be obtained
at www.ICGtesting.com
Printed in the USA
LVHW081057280622
722283LV00004B/27

9 780530 836973